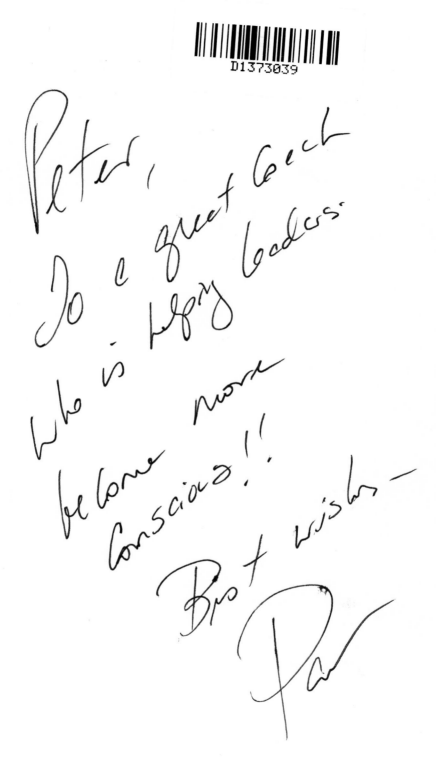

Peters,

Do a great Coech
who is helping leaders
become more
conscious!!

Best wishes —

Dan

TRUE TILT

An Uncommon Quest

Pam Boney

authorHOUSE®

AuthorHouse™
1663 Liberty Drive
Bloomington, IN 47403
www.authorhouse.com
Phone: 1-800-839-8640

First published by AuthorHouse 10/21/2010

ISBN: 978-1-4520-8663-7 (e)
ISBN: 978-1-4520-8122-9 (sc)
ISBN: 978-1-4520-8121-2 (hc)

Library of Congress Control Number: 2010914645

Printed in the United States of America

This book is printed on acid-free paper.

Dedication

To all of the people who are responding to the call of the leader's true journey and transcending to solve the complex problems of today's world with spiritually inspired creativity. Even in our imperfections, we can come together in ways that rise above our individual capabilities. Great virtue is called forth in us when we face challenges that require them. Those who respond with balanced measures of courage, wisdom, resilience and humanity are the true heroes of history and give us a better world to leave to our children.

Acknowledgements & Disclaimers From the Author

NOTE: You will want to read this if you know me.

If you think you see yourself in this book, it will be because of one of my favorite theories in Tilt: we are all capable of the same set of human patterns because we're all made to be fully human – including all aspects of personality. So, you will likely see yourself or parts of yourself in all the characters because they represent all the possible traits of humanity. Some demonstrate virtues and some vices, and the main characters have both – but not to extreme degrees. The evil characters are part of us, too. They remind us what we could become if we lose our moral compass and fall prey to normal temptations because we're unbalanced or out of integrity. Behaving with integrity is not always the easy choice, but it is the one that drives self-respect and growth. It is the divergent path where some go one way and others go another.

Character Disclaimer: None of the characters in this book are solely YOU or solely ME. They are parts of us clarified in a character for illustration. If you recognize yourself, you may want to pay attention to the lessons of that character. One thing that fascinated me in writing the book was how easy it was to write characters who are uniquely THEM and not someone I know specifically. Not even myself. You may think, "Oh, Addie is Pam." Addie's story does start out like my true-life story, yet Addie is NOT me and this was a surprise – a different character who's not very much like me unfolded before my eyes. Yet, she IS one ASPECT of me that I'm only now coming to know. The point is that we move through the development journey and we evolve. We change. We become more because of what we go through. We travel through the four archetypes over and over on our journeys. I was amazed at what came out of me through my writing. I learned that I'm much more complex and rich inside than I ever would have dreamed. I hope all of you will try it yourself for your own journey!

Phrase disclaimer: Some of you may notice I've borrowed something you taught me or a particular phrase you use that's funny. For example, Jean Hauser taught me to "lead where you stand," and my good friend Jeff says "Geez-o-Pete," and Melissa calls my dog "Licorice Lips." So thank you, all my friends and colleagues I've enjoyed over the years, for giving me wisdom, laughter and joy that I could draw from to write this book.

People disclaimer: Only a few characters in this book are real: Yellowmon is truly a boatboy we met on our trip to the Grenadines. Miss Jane-Rose was truly a Matriarch of Mayreau for most of the 19th century and created a utopia there. Brother King, who started the Old Hegg Turtle Sanctuary, is also real and I hope you will donate to his cause. I tried to reach him to be sure it's okay to mention his work here, but never heard back, so I hope he'll see that I'm in awe of his commitment and vision.

Place disclaimer: The settings in the book are real places Dan and I have visited. We had our first kiss in St. Pierre and were engaged in Mayreau. Byahaut is an eco-travel resort owned by a couple (Charles and Sharon) that now live in Virginia. Charles helped me with facts about Byahaut. The remaining places are authentic but many details are made up, so the specific details are part fiction and part real.

Now for the gratitude: Most importantly, I want to express my most heartfelt appreciation for my coach and editor, Mary Bast. Not only is she a great editor who gave me a wonderful experience writing my first book, she is a dear friend and mentor. I would not be the person I am today without our seven-year relationship. Her contributions to the elaboration of Tilt are many. Her gentle support has been the safe harbor where I have been able to birth the Tilt theories and ideas into a manifested form.

I also want to thank my husband Dan who is my great love, my best friend, my business partner, my favorite captain and my advocate. Because of him, I've been able to dive into the various creative endeavors of my life's work — and this book is part of that. By his side, I have been able to explore the world more fully.

Family Gratitude: I want to thank my daughter Amber, who is the greatest treasure of my life. She has become a young woman I admire and respect and a living example of integrity for me, so she and her husband Christopher were part of the inspiration for writing this book. I want to thank my mom, Patricia, for her continuing support and unconditional love, and my stepfather, Jim Adams, for his commitment to my personal growth and wisdom in his latter years. And to all my extended family, siblings, in-laws and more – it is a privilege to have so many wonderful people in my life.

Specific thanks for contributions to Tilt, Inc., founded in 2008: Prior to starting the company marketing Tilt, many people contributed to the work. Paula Page worked side by side with me for years perfecting the first paper version I used to coach leaders in the hospitality industry in the early 1990's. All the many leaders who worked with me in the hospitality industry contributed by allowing me to observe their behavior patterns giving me a rich body of knowledge to develop Tilt.

T. Napier and I collaborated to correlate and validate the items in both our models into four quadrants. Beth Robinson worked with me to categorize the virtues and perform criteria testing. Patricia Adams and Mary Bast both collaborated with me for years to perfect the items, categories and connections across the model. Mary also helped me compare my work to the Enneagram.

I also want to thank Paul Della Maggiora for contributing technical coaching to find the right technologies to turn Tilt into an instrument, Barbara Giemsa for being an early believer and providing a graceful ending to our joint business endeavor so I could pursue my passion more fully. I appreciate Dr. Tony O'Driscoll, who recognized the potential of the Tilt Model and recommended it to the Redhat People Team who became early adapters in 2008. Special thanks go to Delisa Alexander, leader of the Redhat People Team for being our continuing research partner and first believers in the Tilt Leadership Model and Tilt 360 Leadership Predictor.

Most especially, I thank Dr. Bart Craig for being willing to take on the role of Chairman for my Thesis Committee and for doing the number crunching on the validation testing; Jeff Smith, Megan Foutty and Steven Toaddy for contributing to my research thesis; Beth Pisculli, who contributed her energy and enthusiasm to the startup of the business to teach and market Tilt; Evan Lange and Denielle Emans for making all the models and materials beautiful; and finally Ron Wilder for contributing his skills to develop a stronger business strategy for the next stage of growth beyond infancy.

Most importantly, my continuing heartfelt gratitude goes out to the amazing Tilt Team, Practitioners and Providers who teach Tilt all over the world. Nothing happens without the great work you do each day.

As you can see, my blessings and believers are many. I sit in awe of the gifts they contributed to help this creative endeavor come alive.

Pam Boney
August 2010

PART ONE

The Epiphanies

The Phoenix rises out of the abyss.

"The last of the human freedoms: to choose one's
attitude in any given set of circumstances,
to choose one's own way."

- Viktor Frankl

Chapter 1

The evening should have been the pinnacle of her career. As Addie mounted the stairs in the Grand Ballroom to accept the award, she felt awkward in the tight, black, floor-length gown that restricted her movement even more than the skimpy heels underneath. She'd never felt quite comfortable in dresses or with her hair up, but the occasion required it and her hotel had just won the highest award possible in one of the most well known hospitality companies in the world. So she had to look the part. Her team had accomplished the impossible, exceeding performance in all key performance indicators on the company's balanced scorecard.

She was accepting the leadership award for the Top Hotel in the World from the tall and aristocratic Chairman of the Board. Mike Rockwell dripped with charm, smarts and tan good looks. Addie felt weak-kneed as she mounted the marble stairs to the podium.

The room teemed with the luxurious romance of colorful floral arrangements and candlelight bouncing off antique gold chandeliers. Into the far corners of darkness, all she could see were black ties, tuxedoes and shimmering gowns. Was it possible she knew all these people and she was up here on stage? Were those her team members being interviewed, talking about her on the towering screen behind her? The flush on her upper chest betrayed her nervousness and embarrassment. Addie was always uncomfortable being the center of attention and this was a moment where being onstage was unavoidable. Taking care of other people usually kept the focus off of her. Wasn't this why she'd chosen hospitality, to avoid her own emptiness? What was she doing up here? The cameras flashed as she held the heavy Rockwell Trophy in her arm, all smiles in the embrace of the powerful Chairman of the Board. And then, as quickly as it came, the moment was over.

Addie descended the stairs, a crowded rush of chattering colleagues immediately surrounding her, chomping out congratulations, enthusiastic handshakes and rowdy embraces. The rest of the evening was a blur. Addie was swept around the room as person after person offered congratulations. She found herself with no sense of satisfaction, though she'd worked tirelessly for the last two years. Instead, a dark cloud enveloped her consciousness. She desperately tried to avoid something on the edge of her awareness but it was gaining on her. Perspiration rolled down her back as she danced with someone she didn't even know. She had no idea what he'd just said and was at a loss for how to answer. *What am I doing here?*

The room full of people overwhelmed Addie with emotions she'd hoped to avoid, and she longed to escape. When she felt the old familiar pain she knew so well, the only solution was to be alone. That way no one could see past her false bravado and she could stop pretending, a practice that took great effort and drained her of precious energy.

Going out to party in the clubs after the ceremony was out of the question, so Addie uttered apologetic goodbyes and headed back to the safety of her quiet hotel suite. This was her big night in lights but her singular focus was to call her team and tell them what they'd won. Maybe that would help lift her spirits. Unfortunately it was too late to catch the night manager. Instead, the hotel's long time, loyal night auditor, Chuck, was on the other end of the phone.

He responded with his usual lack of enthusiasm to Addie's good news, but he did promise to tell the team first thing in the morning. Addie was sure they'd be thrilled with the news and awed by the irony of earning this prestigious award in a year when they'd worked fewer hours each week (no more grueling 70-hour weeks), focusing on life practices that enabled performance AND balance. The team would be so proud of the accomplishment, mostly because of the many obstacles they'd overcome together. Yet the exhilaration of the historic moment wouldn't have the expected effect on Addie.

She hung up the phone, her mind in utter silence. Sitting awkwardly positioned on the bed, legs dangling, her delicate sandals fell off with a light thud that sounded louder than it should. She had no idea what to do next. *A frightening prospect, for a person who finds her value in moving forward to take care of someone or something.* Staring blankly at the trophy sitting on the parlor table, she let her soul go black with the emotions she'd been avoiding.

Addie was aware of only one thing. She felt as alone as she'd ever felt. It dawned on her that she had no one else to call. Her daughter, Emma, was long tucked into bed, her troubled marriage was all but over, and she didn't have any close friends. Energy was reserved for work, her daughter, and anything else that kept her busy enough to avoid the dark feelings that chased her. She worked all the time and avoided social relationships that required any serious level of commitment on her part. She could call her parents, but they were busy with lives of their own and probably asleep, too. The absence of people who might care about her accomplishment was suddenly and conspicuously obvious.

In that moment of clarity, Addie deeply acknowledged the personal cost of her relentless drive to work more than she should and with a force she was yet to understand. In the silence, a still small voice rang out: "Who is there to care if you win?"

Suddenly the trophy looked too large, too shiny and very, very cold. Instead of success, it represented lost love, broken loyalties, a half-furnished house full of dead plants, a neglected cat and questionable parenting. She sat stunned by the shock, completely present to the pain of loneliness. The trajectory of her life flashed through her mind as she wondered what she'd been so hell-bent to find. What manner of energy propelled her drive for work, so much that it dominated her entire being?

Her daughter, Emma, was the only person she'd let come close enough to see the truth. Most painful of all was the knowledge that Emma could plainly see her ruse. What manner of life was she teaching her beloved daughter to pursue? Her mind flashed back to the last time she'd been late to pick Emma up from dance practice. With tears in her eyes, Emma had wisely asked why work was so important. More important than her. That memory still felt like a dagger in Addie's heart and put the trophy into crystal clear perspective.

As she looked around, the perfectly furnished suite looked surreal. The luxury of the linens and the grandeur of the accommodations were suddenly not very comforting. In the silence of her room, Addie could no longer avoid the staccato of sound in her ears, as loud as a symphony of cicadas screaming in unison on a dark July evening. Yet unlike the peacefulness of a summer evening, this particular sound was maddening, imposing and rising up.

In a coherent moment-of-truth Addie knew what she so desperately needed – a familiar pair of loving eyes, two hands holding her face to wipe away the tears now streaming down her cheeks. She longed for a warm embrace that represented everything she hadn't had in a long time and maybe never would, if she didn't make some changes. This realization gave her a small spark of hope.

The wide gap between who she was at work and who she was in her personal life was a fissure at her center that divided her into two persons. Suddenly she desperately wanted to be whole. She knew she was capable of being more, she just didn't know how to find that path, much less where it would lead.

When it came to accounting or quality or aesthetic design or leading with dignity and respect, she knew about that kind of integrity and lived it. Yet how much was she doing the same in her personal life? She'd coached her team to first place. When was she going to find a strong voice for her own life? Fix the broken promises? Now it was time for her to change. She could not deny it any longer.

The silence in the room had spoken to her, and Addie knew she would never be the same.

Chapter 2

Jim Chandler felt uneasiness in the air. The firm's partners had been in a meeting all day, and through the glass windows across the hall he could see his friend Stephen pacing the room, in a heated discussion. He doubted Stephen could defend him much longer. Jim hadn't been on his game lately and his charm had run its course with the other partners.

No one had said the meeting was about him, but he had a gut feeling it was. Everyone had been strangely quiet around him lately, throwing covert glances in his direction, or vague agreement that bordered on dismissal when he shared his views in creative meetings. The firm had lost two of its biggest accounts in the last six months, and financials were not in the tip-top shape they'd been for the firm's 28 years in business.

As third largest advertising agency in Pittsburgh, its top accounts were easy prey for the two larger firms, who could pick away at their loyal customers, throwing more money at them and eventually winning them over. Jim had been the lead on two accounts that had recently switched over to Dunn, Logan and Brower, the biggest agency in town. Preoccupied with his complicated personal life the last two years, he'd been holding onto the account relationships by the skin of his teeth, when suddenly he realized they were at risk. By then it was too late to save them. The *Pittsburgh Post-Gazette* had recently run a story about the success of the competing agency, rubbing salt into an already festering wound. *All because of his personal problems, his firm was now suffering a decline in reputation.*

He'd lost focus, and no one knew it better than he did. Jim was keeping a secret that was slowly killing him, his obsession with Erin, an intern who'd come back to work full time. He'd been sleeping with her for more than two years and she was asking for promises he could not keep. Juggling the demands of two separate lives had become exhausting.

He loved his wife of fourteen years, Robin, and his kids. But this hadn't dissuaded him from becoming involved with Erin. She'd looked at him the way Robin used to look at him before the kids were born, and he'd found it irresistible. He felt fortunate to have his easygoing good looks, but they only got him into trouble. He knew it was dead wrong to indulge in an extramarital affair, and his conscience was killing him, but he felt he couldn't live without the thrill of being desired.

He rationalized the affair by changes in his marriage. Parenthood had slowly taken its toll on the romance. Robin's energy was always focused on the needs of the kids, so he was the last to have her attention. Despite the loss of intimacy, though, he loved her now in a different way, she was HIS wife and he felt responsible for her. For the kids. And for keeping his commitment to them. So he'd chosen to keep that commitment to his family, yet take what he needed wherever he could get it. He deserved to have a love life. It was only natural to want that. But the guilt was increasing instead of getting easier. Especially now that he'd been exposed and he had to face it with other people. *What's wrong with me that I'd risk everything, all we've built?* The guilt was scorching his insides.

Yet risk it he had. He couldn't help himself, when sassy Erin practically threw herself at him after a business dinner. He hadn't felt like this since his college years at Princeton. He thought he could indulge just a little for the fun of it, and playfully let her pursue him. Once he'd tasted the forbidden fruit, though, he couldn't stop. Now, it was going to cost him everything.

All in the span of a few months, Jim had lost his credibility. Not only was his focus off, his sense of self was missing. He knew it and everyone around him knew it, too. It was the reason for his loss of stature at the firm and at home. His wife sensed things weren't right between them, and at some point his kids, too, had stopped listening to what he said. Joking with the kids and being "good-time Charlie" no longer worked. He was detached. Unable to love. Anxious. Guilty. With lie upon lie he'd weaved himself into a sticky web of his own making.

Unable to speak his mind at all, Jim didn't know himself anymore. The power of his youthful attractiveness was shallow and fading. He'd lost it, that was all. The panic radiating from his midsection was giving him almost constant indigestion. Even the drinks after work failed to relax him anymore.

High school and college life had been so easy. Captain of the basketball team, he'd been popular and always the star. An epicure of life, he was the ring leader in his circle of friends. Voted most likely in the senior class to be successful, no one questioned that his life would turn out great. Quick-witted and intelligent, he had a creative mind and could charm the pants off anyone. *Well, maybe that was where things went wrong.*

Jim had confided in Stephen, who'd tried to talk sense into him numerous times, but Jim hadn't been able to stop. Stephen had confronted him again last week. News of the clandestine relationship had finally made it to the partners and the majority partner was a staunch conservative with strong moral convictions. Jim knew he wouldn't survive the landslide that was about to cave everything in around him.

He put on his overcoat and headed out the door. He had to walk. The icy air cut through his skin, but he was so numb he didn't even feel the cold. He needed a drink and he needed to think. Somewhere off the beaten path. All hell was about to break loose. Today would be his last day at the agency. He would have to explain to Robin. To everyone.

Yet, strangely, Jim felt a sense of relief. He'd once been a man of conscience, and his recent duplicity had not been easy on him. Not so long ago he'd been an idealist with big dreams to change the world of advertising with his novel approach and ideas. He just wasn't very good at following through. He wished he could put his finger on the exact date and time when people stopped listening. He tried to remember the last great idea he'd had for a campaign that ended well. His head pounded with the promise of a migraine.

He couldn't keep face anymore. He was out of steam and no longer desired to be anything but himself. *Sometimes you have to accept your weaknesses and look them dead in the eye.* There was nothing else left. Jim knew he was on the verge of the most important moment of his life.

Entering the bar in the tavern several city blocks away from the office, he sat down and ordered a Scotch on the rocks. Macallan 18. He felt a little better as he watched the bartender pour the sparkling amber liquid over a glass full of ice. Next to him, a man who looked exceptionally successful nodded in Jim's direction. "Bad day, eh? Let me buy you a drink."

Chapter 3

Kit had never lost at anything. Sharp, hungry and smart, she was a tough competitor in any battle of wits. Gazing at the chess board in her boss's office, she gauged his next three moves, then without hesitation made a play that would put him in checkmate in four moves. That is, if he was as predictable as she hoped. She knew his style wasn't as aggressive as others might think. Less than ten minutes later she announced her win and stood up, stretching her arms in the air as if she'd been waiting to get on with it and finish him off.

"Damn you, Kit Laidlaw," Sebastian exclaimed, "You've done it again! I shall be doomed to lose to the wicked redhead in every match!"

Kit fell into the teasing pattern they'd both come to enjoy. "You always let me win, don't you, Sebastian, you old rascal? I think you rather enjoy losing to me."

"No, no, no. You have won fair and square again, Kit, my dear. You've beaten an old man at his own dirty tricks! Well done!" He winked at her, then paused and gave her a sober look. "Sit back down Kit. We have some other business that must be done, and not as pleasant as this game. Have a seat and listen."

The senior partner at a popular Dallas consulting firm named after him, Sebastian was famous for the best sellers that had made him a very rich man. An icon now, he enjoyed being a wise old father to the partners, who all admired and wanted to please him. All but Kit, who mostly played devil's advocate in meetings, even when he was there. She spoke her mind and he tolerated it from her. But never from the others.

"Kit, we are really going to be tested if I take the hotel acquisition project. They're now the biggest conglomerate in the world, it has never been done before, and the cultures in the various companies could not be more different. This one is likely to be extremely complex and potentially tumultuous. I'm concerned it may take us to the limit. We have to let them know tomorrow and I haven't slept well in weeks. If we fail, it could put us under. We're strong and capable, but we've never taken on a project of this size, and our success or failure will be painfully transparent. As a good leader, I need to know what we can handle and what projects to take, especially in this turbulent climate."

"What's to worry about, Sebastian? You know we can handle anything you throw at us." Kit had a comfort with uncertainty and challenges that would put a bull-riding cowgirl to shame. Fear was not part of her vocabulary.

"Now, Kit, don't be so sure of yourself. I've been around a few years longer than you have. Just look at the grey hairs on my head. Besides, I'm the one who has to worry about how we're going to handle the work load. And you know you have a tendency to undershoot the required resources. Prudence is not exactly something your mother taught you, God rest her soul." Sebastian was being unusually cautious.

"Give me the scoop now, Sebastian, and stop worrying about how we're going to handle it. Have I ever let you down? I'll make sure everyone kicks in gear." She looked down at the unfinished chess board, turned it 180 degrees and raised her left eyebrow, moving one rook and inviting him to continue the play. The message? She could beat him from either side of the board.

Sebastian shook his head. "Can't say you have, but there's a first for everyone. Even you might get your butt kicked one day, you wily fox! This is a big one and might just tax us beyond our capacity." His face was tired and drawn. Years of a heavy workload, coupled with too many periods of prolonged stress, had taken their toll.

Kit's impetuous and overconfident nature had not helped. They had to have a serious talk. He knew Kit's certainty was often because she didn't know enough about the situation, wasn't receptive to views from others and was not patient enough to do more homework. His wisdom had taught him that true competence came when you had begun to realize how much you don't know. She wasn't there yet, but then she was still young.

He also knew she didn't take feedback well, no matter who doled it out, and this was a fatal flaw in the business they were in. She'd typically drop into a dramatic routine, first shouting and blaming, then the silent treatment for weeks on end. He didn't know why he put up with it. *How can you be in the business of people-consulting when you are too vulnerable to handle feedback yourself?* He had to appreciate her passion. *She's a fighter, that's for sure.* Yet fighting didn't earn long-term loyalty from customers or employees. It made them want to distance themselves. And this is what he'd noticed happening. He was worried she'd go too far. Maybe she already had.

The storm was about to happen. But he had a plan that might help. Kit had to be at her best to help him pull it off. This was a matter of importance to him personally and he wanted to make a strong statement with the outcome. A public one.

"There's something else I want to discuss with you, Kit. It concerns some noise coming from the ranks. Sit down and let's talk about it over lunch. I'll have Sandy order something in for us."

Chapter 4

There it was again. The depression was back and this time in full force, as if it had a perfect memory. Jean Claude had been a loner for four years now. Or was he that way before? He couldn't remember who he'd been "before." So far, the best he'd learned to do was to cope. Barely. Only enough to do his job and piddle around with his numerous hobbies, but little else. He had no personal life now, nor did he care to. After four years, he was keenly aware that he couldn't move forward. He was a lost soul who'd taken his pain along with him like an annoying, unshakable companion. The carefree life of pleasure he'd enjoyed when he was younger had slipped through his fingers in the passing of one fateful day.

Jean Claude had been working too much when he got the oddly spontaneous notion to take off for the Grenadines on a surprise adventure vacation. He'd always worked hard, but since graduating at the top of his class at Duke ten years before, his practice had grown faster than he knew how to manage. Mergers and acquisitions had proven to be a clever choice if one wanted to practice law at this particular point in history. Jean Claude's personality had not been well-suited for litigation, but he had an exceptional eye for detail and a penchant for grappling with complexity using disciplined personal integrity, a much-desired skill in the complicated business of M & A law. Coming to the States to study law had been an act of rebellion to his family in southern France but, much to his mother's chagrin, he'd fallen for the exchange student who lived with them in his last year of school. He'd followed Jane back to North Carolina to pursue his undergraduate education and was able to get dual citizenship because his mother was also American. He'd chosen well and was happy beyond reason. Until life dealt him a tragic blow.

Jean Claude rarely made it through the night without nightmarish scenes from that day in July. With practiced precision, he punished himself again, thinking back to the details.

His beloved wife, Jane, had been every bit the curious explorer and problem-solver he was. It hadn't taken much to get her to sign up for a SCUBA diving class while he studied for his bar exam, and the two of them had nearly 80 dives between them by the time of the accident. They were in the lower islands of the Caribbean, chasing clues passed down through generations of Jean Claude's family. His direct ancestors had all been sailors, venturing out to sea before they reached full maturity. This passion had been passed down through centuries of wanderlust genetics and Jean Claude had not missed the trait.

His father had passed along tales of his great, great grandmother, the captain of a great sailing vessel commissioned by the king of France to explore the New World in search of spices and other treasures. The stories had been told and retold in his family for centuries, and his father kept a trunk of old maps, documents and treasures under lock and key. Jean Claude had persuaded his father to open the trunk on his 21st birthday and from that day forward had been obsessed by the contents and the clues to a treasure hidden by his ancestor, Captain Jeanne de Sainte Hilaire, a notorious female privateer for the French in the West Indies in the early 1700's. It was told that she'd solved the mystery of great leadership and carved the ancient secrets into the helm's wheel of her ship, *La Bagourt*. Jean Claude was fascinated by her story and determined to find the code she'd written.

On the third day of their trip he and Jane had been in Denniss's Hideaway in Old Wall Village, and heard about a new cave, one they hadn't realized existed before now. They'd explored every cave known to the local population. Yet this one was different. It was under water. *This has to be the one!* They had learned about it by chance. Several young skin-divers drinking at the tavern were boasting about something they'd found in the "Great Underwater Cave" just off the coast on the southernmost tip of Mayreau. Jean Claude and Jane had contained their excitement and prepared for the two-tank deep dive, studying maps of local divers to plan their dive. They checked over all their equipment twice and hired one of the young men to go with them; to be sure they'd find the right cave.

Yinny was a tall, skinny, brown-skinned teen who it was said could skin dive to nearly 50 feet, holding his breath for as long as four minutes. The three of them took off in the wooden dinghy and headed to the dive site off the coast of Mayreau. After anchoring, they rolled off the back of the boat and began descending to the opening of the underwater cave. Jean Claude could still remember, with vivid detail, the feeling of the oppressive mass of water above them as they passed below 80 feet. It also grew darker and darker, despite the midday sun above the surface. An ominous feeling grew, as the two of them followed froglike Yinny to the mouth of the cave. The current was surging and their descent into the cave opening required pointing straight down into the mouth of the cave. Strong kicking was required to push past the cross currents through the opening. On the other side of the cave opening, it was pitch black. Yinny had turned on his forehead flashlight and motioned to Jean Claude and Jane to do the same. An underworld of nighttime sea life leapt to life before them. Creatures like nothing they'd seen in sunlight floated in the secret life of the cave. A shape-shifting octopus scurried across the rock, one ominous eye on the intruders. It should have been a memory to keep for life, and it would be. But for all the wrong reasons.

The three divers made it through the most dangerous part of the dive and switched to their second tanks. Though not finding what they were looking for, they'd run out of time and had to start the slow surfacing procedures, to avoid any possibility of the bends from such a deep dive. They were on their way back to the cave opening, following the safety line left by Yinny, when a loud explosion disrupted their ascent. Yinny, who was closest to Jane, was pushed against the sharp reef coral and began bleeding profusely. Jane's flashlight and mask had been blown from her head and she was giving the hand signal that meant "No air" to Jean Claude as he attempted to re-orient himself. Grabbing the octopus regulator from his own BC, he popped it into her mouth for a temporary reprieve. Then he began frantically problem-solving.

Yinny was obviously incapacitated and barely breathing, losing so much blood he was unable to communicate. Jean Claude took control, pulled them both close to his side and began the swim up to the cave opening. The only light was coming from his own flashlight, which had miraculously stayed in place on his forehead. He figured the explosion had been a blown O-ring on Jane's second tank, so he knew all the air had escaped and the tank was useless. As he pulled all three of them from the cave opening, he yanked the four useless tanks free and let them drop to the ocean floor below. *We'll have to come back for them later.*

The three of them would have to survive the long ascent on two tanks of air. He'd checked the gauges on both tanks, quickly calculated that a very slim margin would allow them to make it. He'd have to risk a faster ascent than was ideal. Yinny was listless and barely breathing from his regulator, so Jane would be okay sharing air from his octopus regulator. They were both small people and would require less air than Jean Claude would, especially given that his effort would carry them up toward the light. He would need his own tank to save them all. Knowing this didn't make the decision any easier. Time passed in slow motion as he clocked the time required at each checkpoint. The air gauge on the two remaining tanks declined steadily and both were in the red zone when they finally reached the 15-foot stop. He would need to wait at least five minutes at this depth to prevent the bends. The closest decompression chamber was in Grenada, and they couldn't be airlifted there in time. He'd have to make them wait the five minutes, taking the chance they'd run out of air but could dash to the surface at the last minute.

Once surfaced, he'd have to locate Yinny's boat and swim with them a long way, because they'd emerge in a different place than they would have according to the dive plan. His BC could not be inflated with no air left, so they'd be without flotation devices, and he worried they'd all drown in the tumultuous surface waves.

As he turned around, the nightmare started. Motioning to Jane to come to the surface now, he saw a large gray mass of motion approaching behind her. A bull shark at least 10 feet long was headed right for Yinny, who'd been bleeding profusely all the way up. Jean Claude had worried about this but hadn't let himself dwell on it. He realized now he'd put his wife in danger by attaching her to Yinny's tank. Then, a big thud as the huge shark bit into Yinny's body, pulling the regulator from Jane's gaping mouth. The look of horror in her eyes had plagued him for four years. He wasn't sure he'd ever be able to forgive himself. He pulled her to the surface and swam the 50 yards to the boat in constant terror of another shark attack. He pushed her on-board first, then dove again without his tank and gear to search for the helpless Yinny, adrenaline pumping through his body until logic told him there was no possibility for Yinny to survive. Tired and drained, he used the last of his energy pulling himself into the boat to go for help.

They were underway to the dock before he realized Jane's leg had been sliced open by the bull shark's razor-sharp teeth. A pool of blood was collecting under her legs. Should he stop the boat to find the injury and stop the bleeding, or should he race to the mainland? He decided to drive as fast as he could. By the time he got her to the island clinic, she'd lost too much blood and was so pale he began to panic and second-guess his decisions. They'd airlifted her to Grenada but it was too late. After a two-day fight, she gave up and passed away in his arms just after midnight.

Jean Claude had never been able to let it go, driving himself crazy trying to figure out what he could have done differently. In the end, it was easiest to blame himself for being there in the first place. His crazy, obsessive adventure to solve the mystery of his ancestor's puzzle. They should not have even been there. He shouldn't have talked her into going. His need to solve the puzzle had been selfish.

The week following Jane's death, he volunteered as crew on-board a sailing vessel bound for the Canary Islands, off the coast of Africa. The captain of the vessel was determined to compete in the Whitbread Around the World, a race to begin in September in Cowes, England. On a desperate whim, Jean Claude saw this as an escape from the nightmare of his circumstances. He couldn't go back home, that he knew. He called his business partner Samuel and relinquished his ownership in exchange for a substantial sum, then set sail for a year, intent on scourging the tortured thoughts from his mind.

PART TWO

The Seekers

Resilience ~ **The call of spirit invites us to ascend, and the Wanderer becomes the Seeker.**

"A mind stretched by a new idea cannot find a way to get back into its previous container."

- Oliver Wendell Holmes

A Divergent Path

Seeker of truth
Dreamer of dreams
Builder of castles
Beacon for those
who dare to expound
on the mysteries within
to bring them to life
and demand countenance
for a new brand of thought…

…joining intellectual endeavor
and spiritual healing
so empowered
that in the end
we are mindful of our impact
and find
we are not in need
of the castle
at all.

Chapter 5

"Are you the Seeker?" A voice spoke to Addie in the corridor of the airport on the way home. "Are you going home, going back to work, or are you going to the Caribbean?" The man behind the voice spoke casually, as if she were making a decision here and now.

"Are you kidding? What kind of choice is that?" Addie asked. "Do you actually know someone who wouldn't choose to go to the Caribbean out of those three?" She still wondered who this stranger was.

"Sure," he said, increasing his stride to catch up with her. He had bronze, tanned skin and long blonde hair knotted up in dreadlocks. His eyes were blue behind round, wire-rimmed glasses, drawing her in with their humor.

"Sure, what?" she asked.

"Sure, I know someone who would choose one of the other two. That would be YOU," he answered with a curious smile. Addie suddenly shivered, but shook it off and gave him a chilly stare.

"Me? Why would I choose such a thing?" she asked, feeling a little too transparent.

"I dunno. You're the one who would choose it." His blue eyes held hers without blinking.

"Well, I am NOT going back to work. I am going to the Caribbean." She stated this matter-of-factly, surprising herself. She hadn't been on vacation in more than four years, but one notch up the challenge pole and she'd go for it. Addie's face flushed from revealing herself, though for some odd reason she felt little shame.

"You'd better hurry!" he snapped, "The plane leaves in 15 minutes. Gate 12. Puerto Rico and then on to the BVIs."

"BVIs, what are they? Kind of like BVDs?" She was playing along now, though for what purpose or with whom, she did not know. Yet she was having a little fun with this quirky guy, so why not?

"Very funny," he said. "I guess you could look at it that way. Only you won't need BVDs. Only a couple of t-shirts, some shorts, flip-flops, a snorkel, mask, fins and a bikini or two will do. Might want some foulies, too, in case it rains. You can buy them when you get there." He grinned, somehow intuiting how much she hated not having a plan. *Another challenge from a stranger who saw straight through her. And what the heck were foulies anyway?*

"You'd better run. I'll take that suitcase and send it to your house. It won't fit on the boat. You'll need a duffel bag. Something that stows easily once you're on-board. Not much space you know!" With that he began running down the corridor.

She yelled after him, "Wait! What did you say your name was?"

"Perspective," he shouted back, "but you can call me Speck. Oh, I almost forgot to tell you. There's a package waiting for you at the service desk in Puerto Rico." Then, in a flash, he was gone.

Addie didn't know where she was going and suddenly wished he'd come back. Yet something about him piqued her curiosity and gave her comfort at the same time. Balanced with just the right amount of challenge, these traits were a perfect magnet for her. What a curious fellow. Weird too. Curiously, she'd trusted the guy with her luggage and was going along with his plan.

What gate had he mentioned? Everything was cloudy and uncertain and at the same time fun, too. She kept walking down the corridor, her legs careening ahead, as if the rest of her would somehow follow if she obeyed. After all, she was feeling rather un-tethered since the conference. She was beginning to wonder if she was imagining things. *Maybe I should head home after all.*

"Attention, all passengers departing for Puerto Rico, the gate has been changed. Repeat, the gate has been changed. All passengers to Gate 12. Boarding all rows. Departing in 15 minutes. Gate 12." The loud airport voice boomed at just the moment she was considering going instead to the gate that would take her home. How did the guy with the dreadlocks know the flight to Puerto Rico was going to be changed to Gate 12? The loudspeaker announcement made her think twice as she considered the crazy possibility of accepting his challenge.

He was right, of course. She never went on vacation, not since the one to Hawaii with her ex and daughter, before the separation. She hadn't been able to tolerate more than two days before getting antsy and wanting to go back to work. She wasn't particularly good at letting go and having fun. Yet now she felt the strange desire to move toward something new, the memory of her loneliness in the hotel suite at the edge of her mind. *If you keep doing the same things, you'll keep getting the same results.* She needed a change of scenery. A change of anything, really.

As she rushed to the gate the attendant winked. "We were looking for you. Weren't sure if you were going to make it. Glad to have you aboard, yes, we are!" She handed Addie an envelope. In it were exactly $808.20 and an e-ticket with her name on it. Addie Duke, seat 12A. Five minutes later, as she was entering the boarding tunnel, she looked back at the ticket agent and asked, "Hey, who left this envelope, a guy named Speck?"

"Oh, no. He told us you'd be coming but the envelope was left by Providence. The practical things always come from Providence when you need them." She looked at Addie as if she should have known that. Addie didn't. Things seemed different today. Like a weird but delightful dream. Not like in the real world where you had to work like hell for everything you got.

Addie gave the ticket agent her boarding pass and found seat 12A, hoping no one would sit next to her so she could spread out and read the paper. She hated it when people wanted to talk during flights. Planes were her only time away from work demands, where she gave herself permission to unwind.

Chapter 6

The flight from Dallas to Puerto Rico was to be several hours long, so Addie hoped to read the paper, catch a movie and take a nap before arrival. The American Airlines 767 was large and promised to be reasonably comfortable, so she figured her plan would be a no-brainer. Rounding the corner of the Jetway, she'd nosed past a very slow, large woman in a yellow dress with a big multicolored shoulder bag clutched to her chest. *Probably had her entire medicine cabinet in it.* The way the woman walked betrayed her obvious pain, carrying her body on feet too small to comfortably handle the weight. As she moved past, Addie glanced away so she wouldn't have to look her in the eyes and feel guilty about passing her in line. The woman reminded her of something she didn't want to think about.

Addie boarded the plane and settled herself into seat 12A, happy to be in a secluded window seat where she could lean her head on the airplane blanket she'd snatched from the overhead bin in first class. She was always cold on planes, so if she planned to have a good nap, she'd need it. *Planes used to have blankets for everyone, not just first class. What was happening to businesses these days that they cut out basic service needs?*

Ready to fly in peace, she settled down to bury her nose in the paper, excited to realize she was breaking out of her comfort zone, headed to unknown places, trusting in the universe. And things were going well. *So far.*

Ten gloriously uninterrupted moments passed by and the flight attendant was encouraging stragglers to get into their seats. Addie loved this part of flight, the anticipation she'd had since she was a kid flying between divorced parents, embarking on a journey to anywhere with the zest of youthful vigor.

She indulged herself in a memory from many years past, recalling when the notion of her future career first became conscious. Twelve years old, on a flight to New York, she became enamored by the business men and women looking ever so important in their black suits and white shirts, reading the Wall Street Journal. Her parents and older brother were always reading intellectual books and debating the issues, so she had a keen mind for business at an early age. By fourteen, she was sneaking behind them and reading copies of her mom's psychology books and not-so-easy fiction. At sixteen, she'd already decided she wanted to be like Dagny Taggart in *Atlas Shrugged* and run railroads.

As it turned out, she would run hotels instead, but the industry would supply the backdrop for a career that completed her dream. Running hotels was exciting in the same ways that running railroads had been during the industrial age. The idea had probably taken form in those adolescent years. She was unbeaten in family monopoly games, strategically buying up hotels and real estate. Once you had the right properties, the game was simply exhilarating. She felt the same way about airplanes. They were taking important people to important places where they would make important decisions. Business was her destiny.

Just then, the large woman in yellow approached and appeared to be looking at the seat numbers above Addie's row. The one person she'd instinctively avoided was now standing before her.

"Ex-ka-yoo-z me" the woman spoke in a pronounced southern drawl. "Could you possibly be in my seat, ta-way-elve A?"

"No, I'm quite sure I have seat 12A." Addie quickly looked away, scrounging to retrieve the ticket she'd tucked into the seat pocket as trash. Sure enough, her ticket was marked 12A, but apparently there was a mix-up at the ticket counter. Agitated, Addie pushed a button and waited for the flight attendant to solve the situation. She could feel resolve rising within her. It wasn't a short flight, and she didn't want to give up her seat.

Just then, tears began to stream down the woman's face. She was sweating profusely and her hands were shaking. Addie felt a little sliver of empathy. *Why in the Jiminy Cricket is she crying over such a thing? Geez-O-Pete.*

The flight attendant stepped up to ask what was going on. Addie explained the problem, and he ran off to check the computer, returning to propose they both sit in row 12 until everyone was seated. *Greeeaaat!*

The woman in yellow plopped down with all her things, spilling over two seats and knocking Addie on the side of the head with her enormous bag. *So much for my cozy little window seat.* Not wanting to encourage a conversation, Addie pulled her newspaper back up over her face until the situation could be resolved.

"I have just had the worst day!" The woman exhaled broadly, ignoring Addie's body language that screamed *leave me alone.*

The woman reeked of gaudy perfume that Addie dreaded would give her a terrific headache. Thinking it would be rude not to respond, she made a punctuated statement, hoping to end any possibility of listening to the details. "Yeah, it's been a weird one for me, too!" She pulled the paper back over her face.

"My brother passed away this week and I've been in Memphis with my family, putting him to rest in the family plot, God rest his soul."

How in the world, do you NOT respond to a full disclosure like that? Why do people need to be so transparent? Addie put down the paper. *For just a moment.*

"All my siblings behaved so badly this week, it made me sad to belong to my family." The woman didn't check to see if anyone wanted to listen to the words now rocketing from her mouth. She explained how so and so was after his money and another someone was rude to his bereaved wife, calling her a gold digger and much more. The stream of words didn't allow for a two-way conversation, so Addie just listened. When the flight attendant came back, the woman was still talking.

"Turns out I can let you two stay in these seats for the flight," the attendant said, much to Addie's consternation. The woman in yellow was delighted.

"That would be just divine! And let me introduce myself. I'm 'Reesie.' That's what my brother always called me, and the nickname stuck."

Divine indeed. Addie tried to ignore her actual thoughts. *It's going to be a long flight.* She was tired and still out of sorts from her own heart-gripping emotions. It was almost frightening to feel the unwelcome emptiness she'd been fighting off for two days.

"Maybe it would do you some good to listen to my story," said Reesie, who acted as if she were reading Addie's thoughts.

Addie surprised herself by asking, "Well, what did your brother do for a living?" She avoided the silly-sounding nickname for this large woman, and hoped to keep this a superficial conversation. Business was her safest category.

"Oh, Dellwood was the CEO of some big hotel chain," the woman went on. "Died suddenly and left his wife a very wealthy woman. Not saying she really cared about the money, you see. She begged him for years to stop being such a workaholic and pay attention to his family. A lovely but lonely woman all those years. Very polished and knew how to entertain all my brother's powerful friends. Kids barely knew their dad. I guess they didn't feel very close to him… probably really angry in the end, because they didn't even want to come to the hospital when he became so sick. Sad, really, because he didn't have any close friends who came, either. Only the people who worked for him came to visit, figuring out how to keep the company going. Sad, really sad. And he was such a nice boy when he was young. I don't think anyone really knew who he was on the inside." The one-way conversation continued as she reminisced about their childhood growing up in Memphis.

Addie was half listening at this point, her mind drifting off to an article she'd read not long before in a hotel industry rag. It highlighted the brilliance of Dellwood Cavanaugh's strategy, which was described as complicated and creative. He had single-handedly engineered the biggest takeover in the industry's history, buying up three of the most prominent worldwide brands and folding them into one company under a large, private equity umbrella. Addie had admired his obvious power and guts, but also felt uneasy when she thought about her own small but extremely successful hotel company being folded under this hotel mogul's leadership. The transition was predicted to begin as early as next quarter. Yet, apparently, their new owner was no longer going to be their new chairman. He'd apparently dropped dead this week while everyone was at the conference, and it hadn't hit the papers yet. His second in command would likely be at the helm next. *What have I heard about him, Seth something?*

"Dellwood sure was young to have been so sick," the woman continued. "Had a pancreatic failure and apparently wouldn't go to the doctor for months to see about his pain. Was on a trip to Europe when it happened last week. Took to the bed fast in some remote hotel and didn't get back up for two days. That's when Emily, his assistant, had him flown home in the company jet, but the prognosis wasn't good. Not good at all. Wasn't much longer and he was gone!" She started weeping again.

Addie thought there must be a lot more to that story but wasn't going to ask any more questions. She flipped through the paper, looking for the story that had to be there. *Why didn't I get a Wall Street Journal instead of a USA Today? Drat.*

Just then, the plane lurched. "Reesie" shrieked and her hand jerked out to grab Addie's. The reality of the woman's presence made real by the touch of her hand, Addie answered from an unfamiliar part of herself. "Just hold on to my hand. Be brave." She said this with an atypical quiet and calm presence. Addie didn't know, then, that holding the stranger's hand and supplying her need for courage would be a catalyst, opening Addie to a side of her self that had been sleeping. For a very long time.

Holding Addie's hand, the woman suddenly fell silent, her body relaxing back into the seat. Her breathing slowed, her tears stopped and her eyes closed.

Enjoying the silence, Addie tolerated the close body contact so foreign to her. It gave her a curious feeling to be touching someone in a moment of desperate need. The plane made its way among the clouds, rhythmically droning along with its sleep-inducing music, lulling them both into oblivion.

Chapter 7

The plane lurched again, pulling Addie out of her fog. Peering at her watch, she realized two hours had gone by. She stirred and shifted in her seat, giving herself an excuse to break the connection with Reesie, whose hand was still clinging to the top of Addie's hand. Their eyes met and Addie saw a surprising gift; a shine of gratitude in Reesie's eyes and a genuine smile. Neither of them had to say anything. Reesie gathered her things, then reached over and pressed a compass into Addie's hand. Made of polished gold, it was obviously very old, but well kept by its owner, because no trace of tarnish could be seen. "That was my brother's," she said, "and I want you to have it. No arguments! He always said it helped him find his way when he felt lost. Somehow, I think it might be useful to you." The other passengers were pushing their way around them, edging forward to the exit, and there was no time to properly admire the gift. So Addie quickly tucked it away in her briefcase, with a smile for the woman, who acknowledged this with a nod.

Addie and Reesie gathered their belongings, then walked slowly together down the Jetway, the older woman moving with a little more bounce in her step than when she'd boarded. When she turned in the opposite direction in the terminal, Addie suddenly wondered about her full name.

As if knowing Addie would ask, she was ready with an answer. "Receptivity. My name is Receptivity." She turned and stepped onto the escalator leading away from Addie, as if her job was done.

"What's with the strange names?" Addie asked aloud, but talking to herself.

I'm probably tired and just need a good night's sleep. She hadn't slept well at the conference, wrestling with the sheets coming loose from the badly-made hotel bed.

As she made her way toward the gate heading to The British Virgin Islands, known as the BVIs, she felt a bit of sadness. Instead of pushing it away, Addie knew she needed to sit with it. She was beginning to notice a few things about herself she hadn't noticed before. More importantly, she was beginning to notice more about her surroundings. As she registered the events of the last ten hours, she became aware of something different about the people around her. Everyone seemed so busy, and their conversations so strangely inconsequential. A fellow walking next to her was arguing about lawsuits with the person at the other end of his cell phone. His end of the conversation struck her as argumentative and ridiculous. *What does he hope to accomplish by being such a jerk?* Everyone seemed to be sleepwalking, unaware of the ludicrous nature of their troubles.

Suddenly she had the distinct thought that she should look up at the arrivals display, and just then saw "Now Arriving, Miami" flash on the screen. Looking down the walkway, she noticed people pouring into the terminal from that flight. A familiar, rugged-looking man with light brown hair was headed in her direction as if on a collision course. *Do I know him?* Tie off and jacket on his arm, he looked as tired as she felt. *Jim, I think. Marketing guy.* There was something she liked about him, if she remembered correctly. *Bit of a pushy and overzealous sales type, though. Teetering on arrogant, but very persuasive. Oh, never mind. It doesn't matter.* He bumped past and headed down the corridor with a lingering glance at Addie as he hurried by.

Addie headed behind him in the same direction. Turning on her iPod, she found the song she wanted and it lightened her step. For the first time in a while, Addie felt herself laughing on the inside at the thought of a new future, knowing it could go anywhere. It wasn't like her to be so adventurous. Here she was traipsing off into the sunset, all because some stranger had challenged her. *Boy, I sure am a sucker for a challenge.* Nonetheless, she felt a tug of panic, wondering if she may have been foolish to jump on that plane. The broken record in her head, however, repeated *you don't get different outcomes if you keep doing the same things.* So, she turned her thoughts to a new destination and started looking for the gate.

Chapter 8

"Adelaide Duke, please report to the service desk. Ms. Adelaide Duke, we have a message for you at the service counter." The loudspeaker in the airport was blasting her name so loudly it reminded her of being called to her elementary school office. She'd been in trouble a lot then, for talking back and for general rabble-rousing. Subtle rebellion and getting away with it had been a favorite childhood strategy. Her mother had speculated, wisely, that Addie enjoyed being in trouble. She'd designed ways to avoid the big trouble she could get in if she didn't keep it under wraps by sabotaging herself on the little things. A weird strategy, but it seemed to work for her.

The service desk was just around the corner from the diner where she'd grabbed a quick BLT sandwich.

"Yes, I'm Addie Duke. I was being paged?" She corrected her name to the shorter version that didn't carry the odious memory of being scolded by her mother or the school principal.

"Ah yes." The clerk handed over an envelope taped to the outside of a rather sizable package. "That will be $808.20. It's a C.O.D. package." Only then did Addie remember the envelope she'd been given in Dallas. In it was a money order for $808.20, which she pulled from her briefcase and handed to the service attendant. "Well, isn't that all neat and tidy. Makes it easy for me, no change or calling to get approval. Have a nice day!" The clerk filed the check in her drawer and winked at Addie. *Weird. People sure are winking a lot lately.*

Addie carried the package into the Admirals Club and found an unoccupied armchair. The envelope on the outside had a return address from a company called Tilt, Inc. and a division located on St. John Island, next to the British Virgin Islands. The tagline was The Tilt Academy for Leadership. Having never heard of this, she opened the package and began pulling out its contents. First there were three polo shirts, two t-shirts and a duffel bag with the "Tilt" logo. Sperry boat shoes in her size, along with a few other small items. Four pairs of white shorts, and strange white leather gloves with thick gray pads in the palm and the fingers cut out. She wondered if she'd been invited to a golf outing at the Tilt Academy. A decent B level golfer, she began to feel excited. Golf would be good for her right now. Maybe this was a surprise reward trip for the award she'd accepted at the conference, some secret plan worked out by the HR department.

She tore open the envelope and began to read the document. The heading was "Tilt Sailing Adventure" by the Tilt Academy for Leadership. *Sailing school! Oh no. This is obviously a mistake. I'm terrified of sailing and get murderously seasick.* On the last reward trip she'd won to St. Thomas, Addie had eaten some spicy food and gone for a sunset sail. After the first five minutes she had to lie down at the rear of the catamaran and hang her head over the water, retching fish-food the entire trip. She remembered wishing she could just jump off, drown and end the misery. She'd not stepped foot on a sailboat since. Cruise ships and fast boats were okay, but sailing? *Good grief, I'm the one who gets carsick from sitting in the back seat.* There had to be some mistake. Addie felt clammy with fear.

"Calling all rows, calling all rows, now boarding the last call for Tortola, BVI, Gate 48. Last call for Tortola, Gate 48," boomed the loudspeaker, suddenly giving her a headache. *What am I getting myself into?*

Too far along the path to somewhere, she decided she'd better find out if this was a business reward trip, then deal with the issue of sailing when she got there. Confident she could talk them into switching her activity to golf, she thought she may as well go along to the islands and find out more when she got there. *If it's a reward trip, then for goodness' sake, I should be able to have some control over the reward I want.*

Boarding the plane, Addie nestled into a front seat of the small commuter and finished reading the paper she hadn't finished on the previous flight. Before she knew it, she was deplaning at the colorful Beef Island Tortola airport, complete with free-range chickens and a Tiki hut over the baggage loading zone outside, where she claimed her new possessions.

The jaunt in the taxi to her destination resembled Mr. Toad's Wild Ride, her favorite Disney attraction. The driver sped toward Road Town past thickets of trees, screeching around corners with virtually NO visibility, through winding streets that reminded her of video games her daughter played as a small girl. The island was British, so she kept reminding herself he was actually on the correct side of the road, but she couldn't help the automatic yelps from popping out of her mouth. She held on for her life, terrified but too embarrassed to say a word. She wondered why appearances mattered more than the small amount of bravery required to speak up to the crazy driver. *People are ridiculous. Especially me.*

They headed across the island to pick up more passengers and then to Soper's Hole, where the Tilt Leadership Academy apparently had a satellite office at the marina. The sun was dropping into the horizon across the sparkling water of the Sir Frances Drake Channel, painting the sky a multitude of colors. Tall palm trees swayed in the wind, framing the aqua water with a fringe of green. As they rounded the last 90-degree turn in the tiny road, even more spectacular scenery stretched out before them, and she was overwhelmed with gratitude to be here in this strange place. She used to paint scenes like this – the endless canvases of a young girl's imagination, filled with big visions of the future. She'd loved painting seascapes and sailboats when she was young, a memory she wanted back, despite its painful nature. *Where is that girl now? Where has she gone through the years?*

Addie noticed local foot traffic, small shacks, trash, a brick wall with graffiti and even a brown and white goat running in the parking lot of a small Rite Way grocery store. A stark contrast to the scene she'd witnessed just moments before, and she was struck by the polarity. *How utterly intriguing.* She'd seen such scenes in St. Thomas years before, but today it seemed so real and different. The clarity of the present moment flung her into connection with the world around her. The sights, smells, sounds and warmth of the breeze were exhilarating. Life teemed here with raw energy and pulsed with the truth of humanity in a way that made her want to engage.

The wild taxi driver rounded the circle drive at the marina and screeched to a halt. She'd forgotten to get cash at the airport and was scrounging in her wallet to find a twenty when he said, "It's all taken care of by Tilt. Have a wonderful sail!" There was that word again. Sail. She had to admit; the *idea* of sailing was romantic. It was just that problem of seasickness. She'd straighten that out in the morning.

Unpacking in the colorful little island motel room was easy. Addie was used to the grandeur of hotel suites, but this tiny charming place was just what she needed. *It doesn't remind me of work.* She had her new duffel, and always kept a small amenity bag in her briefcase, so she was equipped for the adventure. She wasn't much on makeup and only needed the four things she kept in the small bag – pink lip-gloss, mascara, a brow pencil and a powder base to smooth out the splash of small freckles on her nose. Washing her face, raking a brush through her long, unruly brown hair and changing into shorts and Tilt polo, she finally began to relax. The noises at the Tiki Hut Bar near the pool sounded inviting. She was ravenous and ready for a drink.

Addie donned her new boat shoes and headed down to the bar, nosing up to the circular counter and beginning her usual banter with the help. "What's the poison of choice here?"

"Ah, dat would be de Pain Killer" the bartender bounced back. "Bess drink der is, ta be sure, and yoo kin only get 'er in the islands." He continued with a lesson on the history of rum and nutmeg in the islands. "Sposed to take away all yer worries gyrl," he chuckled.

That is the most delicious island accent I've ever heard. "No way! There's no rest for the wicked!" Addie enjoyed giving people hints about things that plagued her, and humor was a great way to deal with the damned buggers.

"Ah, but you look rapp'd up-tite, if I say so ma-self. You be a-changin if you stay on de island, yeah. Can't be up-tite here. No way, mon. You drink up dis here Pain Killer 'n ev'rythin will go good! Soon you kin see. Mellow you out, it will." He turned to his duties on the other side of the counter, giving Addie a little space to take in her exotic surroundings.

She pulled the tie from her hair, which sprang free from its prison, falling halfway down her back. It had been a long day. A long week or two, really, leading up to the conference. Her hotel team was well-developed and could run the hotel without her these days, so preparing them for several weeks of her absence had been easy. Her daughter, Emma, was packed off to her grandparents on her daddy's side, for a month of summer in the mountains. The cat was being taken care of by the neighbors and would be madder than a hornet when Addie got home, but she couldn't worry about that.

For the first time in ages, she felt free from the lists of her own making. Not a particularly comfortable place for a person who needs to have things to do, but taking in the scenery around her was starting to affect her whole being. She was warming up, coming to life. She could feel the pulse and rhythm of island life penetrating her well-laid boundaries and seeping slowly beyond them into her DNA.

"You here for the sailing adventure, too?" The question came from a table behind Addie. She turned to see a woman with a wild mane of dark red hair, sitting with a Pain Killer in front of her. She had a sublime, artsy, bold style blended with mischief and just-over-the-edge confidence. It was a trait Addie admired and wished she had for herself. But it didn't seem she'd been doled out the right genes. Insecurity and worry, hidden under false bravado, was more her style.

"Yeah," Addie said. "I guess so." She noticed this woman was wearing the same Tilt polo she was wearing. There was a man at the table, too, with the familiar attire.

"Well, come on over and join us, will you? Kit Laidlaw," the red-haired woman said, quickly offering her hand. It was dry and she had a good solid handshake, Addie noticed with pleasure.

"Addie. Addie Duke." Looking eye to eye for a short connection, Addie liked Kit immediately. She always wanted confident women as friends. The stronger-willed the better. She grabbed her drink and headed for their table without a second thought.

"Hello there," said Kit's companion. This was the man Addie had seen in the Miami airport. "My name's Jim Chandler. Have we met before?"

"Jim, how crass! Is that some kind of pick-up line?" Kit joked.

Addie decided to save Jim, giving him an opening to explain. "No, I think he's right. I saw him in the airport a few hours ago and thought the same thing."

"Now I remember. I saw you, too. We've crossed paths somewhere else, though. I'm certain of it. What do you do, Addie?"

"Hotel business, General Manager of a hotel in Virginia. Just came from our annual conference in Vegas."

"Hmmm, well I'm in the advertising business, Creative Director for an agency in Pittsburgh. Maybe we've pitched your company. Who is it?" He threw back the last of his Pain Killer and nodded to the waitress for another.

"Stanton Suites, a small company based out of Memphis. Just got bought by a large conglomerate though, so maybe you're more familiar with Pyramid International?"

"Yeah, Stanton, sounds vaguely familiar. Don't think you went with us, but I do remember I had some good ideas for you. Too bad it didn't work out." He seemed genuine in his remarks. Addie liked him and his easy way. *Would have been fun to work with him on the campaign.* She'd been past-President of the Southeastern Marketing Co-op for the company, so they'd crossed paths in the corporate offices at some juncture.

Addie turned to Jim's companion. "What do you do, Kit? And where are you from?"

"Oh, I'm from Dallas. Stratus Consulting. Big Texas outfit that helps companies with culture alignment after mergers and acquisitions. Senior Project Lead for major takeover endeavors. I love a tough assignment, so I oversee the really nasty ones, at least from a culture standpoint. Alignment's not always a popular process." She continued explaining the need for her work.

Addie admired Kit's strength of purpose and obvious certainty she was good at her job. Addie never quite felt that way herself. Even with a trophy being shipped home, as she spoke.

"Ugh!" Jim interrupted. "Mergers and acquisitions. My worst nightmare. I managed an advertising account for a company going through a merger. It was so painful it makes my head hurt to think about it. I'm going to need another Pain Killer, I can see that!"

Addie liked the crinkles at the corners of Jim's eyes, probably the result of frequent smiles. *Crinkles on faces are the ever-growing telltales of what lies beneath the surface.* She was horrified by Hollywood faces with so much work done they'd begun to look like ceramic dolls with no personality or character. Jim had good crinkles.

Kit quickly picked up that Jim was in no mood to continue the topic. "Well, I'll spare you the details, then. I can see you've experienced the possible collateral damage."

"I'm afraid I have to agree with Jim for the time being," Addie said. "We've just been acquired by a huge company and I don't give it much hope of success." For the first time, Addie was expressing her true beliefs about what she'd face when she got back to work. The rumors had already started rumbling at the conference and she was not looking forward to a second round of blending cultures. They'd merged with another hotel company three years earlier and the experience had been so ugly the stock plummeted and made the company vulnerable for a takeover. Right now, Addie would not think about it. She was having too much fun.

"I see all of you have met one another already," said a voice from behind. A fellow approached the table in the same polo all of them were wearing; only under the word "Tilt" was "Team Coach."

"Ian Brantley, your host," he offered in a charming British accent, with warm handshakes to all three. "Welcome to the BVIs and to The Tilt Academy. Marine biologist and sailor. Team coach for the Tilt Academy and captain of our ladyship, the *True Tilt*. Your sailing vessel and home for the next few weeks!" Ian was the picture of vibrant health and well-being, with strawberry blonde hair and very pale skin, appearing golden only because of its generous spattering of freckles. He was tall and muscular, so there was no question he was all man, despite the soft hair that played loosely around his angular face.

This might be okay after all. Addie instantly liked Ian, enough to brush aside the fear in the pit of her stomach when she thought of seasickness. She ordered another Pain Killer. *I'll simply have to get over it.* This situation was adding up to something interesting and she didn't want to miss out.

Ian made it all sound so romantic. Not in a guy-meets-girl way, but with a worldly, adventurous approach to life. The utter romance of the ocean, the sand and the stars had always captivated Addie's imagination. She thought back to how much she'd loved the beach as a young girl, how she could sit for hours looking out to sea, dreaming of foreign travel. She longed for the girl who painted seascapes, wrote poetry and love songs to play on her guitar, who yearned for adventure. *Where have those dreams gone? And why do I keep thinking about this lost girl?*

Ian was chatting in his charming, tea-and-honey accent and – lost in her own thoughts – Addie was missing the conversation. She jogged her meandering brain back into the present moment.

"Jolly good, then, we're all off to a fine start. Making friends already, I see! Don't drink too much, though, because there's homework before our debriefing tomorrow at 7 a.m. sharp. You have a book about sailing basics and quite a lot of sailing terms to memorize. There will be time to work on this when we're underway, but you'll be expected to carry your weight on the team, so learning on the fly is essential. We know you're all the brightest of the bright, so there should be no problem, but please take this seriously. You never know what you might encounter when at sea. The dangers are just as real as they were hundreds of years ago, so you must be alert at all times and pay close attention to your surroundings. Your directions are in your rooms and the debriefing room is over behind the BVI dive shop. You'll have a list of provisions to round up after the debriefing and must check out of your room and move on-board the *True Tilt* by 10 a.m. Don't let yourselves get sucked into 'island time' mode, because we have a journey ahead of us. We leave port at 11 a.m. tomorrow, so see you at sun-up." Ian opened nothing to discussion. He looked each of them in the eye, assuring himself that each had heard him. With that, he smiled broadly, waved his hand and was gone.

Addie could see her new companions were as surprised as she was. "Does anyone know what's going on and why we're here?" She knitted her brow in confusion.

"No way" said Kit. "I was headed to a short consulting gig in D.C. when our senior partner called me to a meeting and said plans had changed and I was to jump on a plane and head here. In a month we have to start work on the biggest takeover contract in our company's history. So I'm surprised to be sent here myself. What about you, Jim?"

"Me too," Jim chimed in. "My best friend thinks I'm going through some kind of mid-life crisis and packed me off to 'think about it.' Had his assistant give me a ticket here with no other explanation, and now here I am. Beats the hell out of me. We have a mountain of work to do back at the office and truth is, I think he's kind of off his rocker to send me to some kind of vacation at this point in time. Been thinking I might be off my rocker, too. Weirdest things happening lately..."

"Like people with strange names?" Addie felt right in sync with Jim.

"Yeah, you too? I met a gal named Diligence, of all things." Jim recalled the serious, dark-haired woman who'd visited his office the day before, and who'd made an offhand comment that sent chills down his spine. He didn't like admitting he was potentially hurting the firm's credibility by his lack of personal discipline. And then there was the guy in the bar. The one who told him a story he'd never forget. A man named "Integrity." *Who would have a name like that?* Jim remembered being quite uncomfortable in the presence of this man called Integrity. Made him squirm just thinking about those probing questions and the way the man had looked him square in the eye, waiting for an answer.

"Well of all things, me too!" said Kit. Exhaling broadly, she relieved herself of pent up anxiety that had been frustrating her in one long tirade. "Met a guy in the Dallas airport who told me his name was 'Consideration'. He made an observation about something I did in the security line that was kind of unnerving. The day before, my sitter had called in sick and I had to rush to pick up my kids after school. They were so crazy in the car we almost had an accident, so I was frazzled. We stopped at Starbucks so I could send out a proposal on time, so I promised them chocolate mochas. While I was there, the boys got into a screaming fight and my daughter started crying. A woman I didn't know smiled at me and said, 'Our children are the mirror of what we need to change about ourselves.' She said it while smiling, of all things!

Said her name was 'Trust' and that she was a child psychologist. Said that if I would look at my own reliability and integrity in the way I interact with them, my kids would respond in kind and stop acting out to get attention. And I'd just heard the same story from the senior partner at our firm, who told me I had similar issues with the team and to be ready for the consequences if I didn't change my actions. It was the worst day of my life! Who do these people think they are?" Kit wasn't about to tell them the details of *that* last interaction because it hurt the most. The sting of it was still so raw. To add to it, Sebastian had never given her such strong feedback and it wasn't sitting well with her. She was furious, her mind racing with arguments in her defense. She could feel her pulse gaining speed. *I will give him a piece of my mind when I get back. He's not so perfect himself…*

"How interesting." Addie felt better, now that she wasn't the only person who'd experienced quite a strange day. They were all having different reactions to it, but the clues were there. A pattern was emerging, and she'd figure it out. She loved puzzles.

"I have something that may be helpful," Jim said, pulling an old-looking parchment from his briefcase. "A guy on the plane gave me a very interesting map. Maybe this will give us a clue about where we're going. It looks ancient, and not all of it is readable, but it seems to lead to some kind of treasure marked on it."

As Jim started to unroll the map onto the table Addie thought it might be wise to do this in private. Though she could flip from caution to risk-taking in a heartbeat, right now, she had an instinct for caution. "Wait, Jim, if this is something important and it is a map that leads to some kind of treasure, then let's find some privacy first." She looked around the bar.

"Good idea," agreed Kit. "Let's go over to my room."

As they signed the bar bill, Addie noticed a few people looking at them with interest. The guy in the corner with the bad complexion and dour expression made her feel uneasy. He was watching them too intently and she was glad to have an excuse to move out of his line of sight.

Kit led them to her room across the courtyard and they organized themselves around a small parlor table with a cheap light fixture hanging above. One light bulb peered from the bottom of the unprotected plastic fixture and rocked back and forth, throwing shadows on the map. Kit pulled a small flashlight from the duffel so they could see well.

So old it crinkled as Jim opened it, the parchment was a map of the lower Caribbean. It was penned in black ink with green markings that looked like anchors and small red crosses that seemed to be milestones at various locations. On the bottom of the map, positioned at the lower end of the Caribbean arc, was a Skull and Bones. Its menacing artistry was meticulous. Whoever had drawn it was a masterful scribe. Small notes on the outside edge of the map described clues to find a cave where the treasure was marked. At the bottom of the map in large letters was an inscription in elaborate cursive, difficult to make out in the light.

"I can't figure out what this says entirely," said Jim, squinting in the light and taking the flashlight from Kit.

> *With the might of a thousand pinions will the treasure be found, but no other way. Without the treasure, there is only death and misery. Woeful be the Seekers who turn back from the journey because their souls are blind to the yearning of the call. To be caught unawares is the fate of a fool. Godspeed and good fortune favor the BOLD, which choose to balance their sails. First by ballast and then by the Tilt. Full sails require True Tilt and this, alas, is only possible after traveling to East, and West, North and South. A full 360 degree turnabout, and then the treasure is theirs for the taking.*
>
> *Captain Jeanne Claude de Saint Hilaire*
> *Witness: Nathaniel Frances Drake*
> *Witness: Nicolai Le Clerc*
> *August 1718*

"Fascinating!" Kit leaned in and pulled the map in her direction to look closer. "We've been given a treasure map and we must be going on a treasure hunt. I'm sure Ian will explain everything tomorrow!" Adventure was Kit's personal elixir. She'd been given a little something on the way here, too, but she wasn't about to let on about it, preferring to lay low until she could figure out how it might give her power. There might be an advantage to holding back for the right timing. She loved having a trump card in her hand. *Makes things a lot simpler to put the odds in your favor any chance you get.*

Jim went on to point out a few more minor details in the map, then suggested they all get a good night's sleep and find out more about what was going on at the morning briefing.

Kit had taken a call from the office on her Blackberry and was talking loudly, busily solving someone's problem.

Feeling the weight of the day slip up on her, Addie gladly agreed with Jim's suggestion, waved goodbye and headed back to her room. She intentionally avoided her own iPhone. Her only desire right now was to escape from this crazy, unfolding fantasy world.

The door to her room creaked open and, as she slipped inside, the large palm on the other side of the sidewalk swished loudly in the wind, making her jump. Looking over to the landscaped line of bushes ten feet away, she saw a dark-haired cat running in the other direction. *Must have scared it out of its hiding place.* Locking the door quickly, she changed into one of the t-shirts and slid between the sheets. Addie had never felt a more comfortable bed. Probably because she was bone-tired. Pondering the events of the day, she vaguely recalled "Speck" asking her if she was "the Seeker." Seeing those words again on the map was a little unsettling. It was an old map and probably had nothing to do with her. The thought that there might be a connection lingered in the corners of her mind as she drifted off to sleep.

Chapter 9

Situated near the rows of gleaming white sailboats was a small room with a round table of rough-hewn wood at the center. The sign over the door said BRIEFING ROOM so Addie peeked in. Aside from the table, all she could see was a salt-speckled map of the Sir Frances Drake Channel surrounded by the British Isles. The air felt balmy and warm for such an early hour and she was already hot. A steady stream of activity on the docks made her aware they were not the only vessel due out of port today. Strapping young dockhands in white shorts loaded mountains of provisions onto the wide catamarans. In the distance, she saw an intriguing, large vessel tied to the end of the dock. She was exhilarated and longed to explore these surroundings, so different from those she was used to.

Delighted that she'd awakened early enough to finish breakfast well before 7 a.m., and finding no one in the briefing room yet, she decided to roam the docks before the meeting. Addie's stepdad had been a sailor and taught her a thing or two about boats when she was growing up. She was the only girl and the only one interested in fly-fishing and sailing. She loved both, loved sports that had history and required artistry in their practice. But she had only sailed on lakes. Sailing on oceans was quite another thing!

Addie enjoyed a cup of strong coffee as she strolled along the dock. The boat names were fascinating and carried the names of the home ports where the owners must live. *True Grit*, from Charleston, South Carolina and *Not Guilty*, from Memphis, Tennessee were two of her favorites. Most of the boats appeared to have the same French maker. Beneteau was the brand of choice. Nice crafts, but they all looked a little too much the same for her tastes. With an artist's eye, she longed for more unique boats, noteworthy for their classic lines like those she painted when she was a kid. This fleet was a sea of white gelcoat, except for the big one that drew her eye to the end of the long B dock. As Addie made her way over to her, she began to notice how long and luxurious she was. Miles of polished toe-rail topped off the dark blue freeboard and stretched out in front of Addie as she approached the most stunning boat in the marina. She didn't know much about the particulars of sailboats, but she knew quality craftsmanship when she saw it.

"She's a beaut, isn't she?" a deep, liquid voice came from behind her. Turning, she almost ran into the man lounging behind her. "I've never seen a Hinckley Sou'wester 70, and she's new in the Tilt Fleet so I thought I'd come down and see her myself." He openly admired the vessel behind her. "They have a preference for yachts built in Sweden by Hallberg-Rassy. Amazing yachts with sleek, modern design, but this one, she's a true classic built by the finest builder in the U.S. There's something about them. Looking forward to crewing her for sure! She's about as fine a boat as I'll ever be acquainted with up close and personal. Got in late last night and found some dockhands cleaning the teak, so I talked them into letting me take a tour on-board. You been on-board her yet?"

"No, can't say I have. Just got here myself last night and still trying to figure out why I'm here. In fact, I'd better get back to the marina for the briefing." Addie said this rather quickly, matching the quickness she was feeling in her breath. This man had the thick, black hair and winsome good looks of a Spaniard or Frenchman. Definitely European, but with American clothes. Blue eyes and a tall, thin frame. A white oxford cloth shirt with causally rolled-up sleeves and faded cargo shorts with rainbow flips completed the picture. She wasn't breathing and was about to choke on her own dry throat if she didn't get some water, and fast. Escape was all she could think of. A tangle of extra emotions was the last thing she needed right now.

He nonchalantly waved goodbye, barely looking her way, his attention so steadfastly drawn to the sweeping lines of the 70-foot Hinckley. "Catch you later," he said casually.

Entering the briefing room, Addie noticed Kit, Jim and Ian were already there and reviewing some paperwork together.

"Come on over here, Addie," Ian said in a welcoming tone. "We're reviewing the weather-fax to see if ole Mother Nature is tending to our favor today. Appears we do have a good window of weather and can take advantage of a solid southwest trade wind at fifteen knots for our departure later today. Looking good so far!"

"Briefing of the chart plan starts in ten minutes" said Jim, acting as though he knew exactly what was going on. Worrying that she'd missed some important communication, Addie asked if they would at some point be discussing their purpose for being there.

"Ah, but that's the big question, isn't it?" said Ian, chuckling. "You can't always know what life will bring next, now can you?"

Just then the door creaked open again and in walked The Dreamy Frenchman himself. Addie had given the good-looking man on the docks a name that would minimize his impact on her by adding a little internal humor. "Ahoy there, mates," he said as he strode into the room. "Looks like we have a good day to set sail!"

"Indeed we do, Jean Claude," agreed Ian.

Oh my, he is French after all, Addie thought, chagrined at the irony.

Ian continued, "Welcome to the BVIs, old friend. I was surprised to see your name on the roster again, but very pleased indeed, J.C. You're the perfect addition to this particular trip's challenge. Glad to have you back, for sure!" Ian slapped ole Dreamy right on his very solid shoulders, like they were best of pals. Addie's nerves jumped around in her skin. She envisioned barfing in front of ole Dreamy. "Now that we're all here, let's get down to business, shall we?"

Crowding around the small table, they waited for Ian's lead and began to look over the documents it appeared they'd be signing. Making swift of the liability waivers, Ian dug right in on the charts and began to explain the navigation plan. They would set sail that day and head south for the lower Caribbean for a week-long run. Their destination, at least for the time being, would be an island called St. Vincent, just north of Grenada. They'd be sailing 24 hours a day with very few stops along the way, only to dip in for fuel, water and provisions. One official stop was planned at St. Pierre in Martinique, almost three-quarters there.

Addie was beginning to sweat, droplets sliding down her chest inside the polo. Just when she was thinking about bowing out with some kind of lame excuse, Ian addressed the issues of hydration and seasickness. He explained that most people get seasick and he'd prepare them for how to deal with the "darn bugger." He said the first twelve hours were the worst. After that they'd have their sea legs. Addie was startled to see she wasn't the only one concerned about the dreaded sea malady.

"You'll all be expected to stand your watch at the helm at the appointed shift, even if you're feeling ill. You should bring your water jug and your 'barf' container with you everywhere you go onboard until you get your sea legs."

A giggle escaped Addie's lips as Ian said this, but when he cut his eyes over to her, they told her he wasn't kidding and this was all part of the bargain. *What am I doing here?* The panic was again slipping back up into her throat.

"Now, for the fun part," Ian continued. "We draw names for bunks and for crew roles." He pointed to small pieces of paper folded up in neat squares and tucked in a conch shell in the middle of the craggy wood table. "Who wants to go first for crew roles?"

Jim jumped on the chance to be first. Opening the first square, he announced he'd be the navigator. Ian indicated to Jim that he'd put Jean Claude in charge of teaching him how to use the chartplotter, radar and weather-fax. Jean Claude obviously had some experience sailing and nodded in agreement. Next Kit drew the role of first mate and Ian explained the responsibilities that would make her Ian's right hand in most maneuvers. Jean Claude drew the galley responsibilities, which left Addie with cleanup duty. *Chief Deck Swab. GREEEAT. That will be appetizing on a bad stomach.* Addie chided herself for not being more assertive. *Geez O Pete, I should have drawn first and maybe I would have had better luck. What a ninny!*

"Last but not least, let's talk about our final destination," added Ian, with quite a bit of animation. "We're headed to a small island in the Grenadines, about half way to Grenada. Lowest part of the Caribbean Islands, so it's a seven-to ten-day haul to get there, depending on the wind direction and weather. Our objective is to solve a problem that's recently presented, and time is of the essence. A decision must be made before November 1st. You have each been selected because of your expertise, but more importantly because this is a high-stakes decision and someone trusted that you are the right team to advise the local government on Mayreau. Any questions? I hope not, because that's all I can tell you at this time. It's highly confidential. You must all commit to keeping confidence on this matter until we can get there and assess the lay of the land. No emails or cell calls about the topic. This mission is of importance to a lot of people."

Ian looked at each of them earnestly, seeming to reassure himself they'd all heard him loud and clear. He was not going to fill in the gaps any more than he had, that was also clear. He reviewed a few "Rules of the Crew," including such statements as "If you see it, take care of it," and "Safety comes before pleasure and comfort," and "Two people on deck at all times," and "If at sea you MUST be tethered to the deck with safety lines." These were not rules of engagement Addie was accustomed to. She was intrigued with the strict nature of life at sea.

With that the briefing was over, and the crew was dismissed to collect their duffels, shop for provisions with a specific list and pick up the dive gear waiting for them at the BVI Dive Shop next to the marina. With the task list in hand and the express purpose of their task to assist in some important way, Addie began to feel more at home with the situation. She liked forward motion attached to doing something important. This was the salve she needed to pave the way for a journey of the unexpected.

The more she learned about Ian, the more she relaxed. He was definitely organized, clear and self-assured in his plans. She was beginning to realize they were in good hands with their captain. He was a good leader indeed, and she felt safe.

Chapter 10

Aboard the *True Tilt*, the first tasks were assigning bunks and stowing duffel bags. Jean Claude was familiar with the sailboat, so Ian assigned him the task of drawing for bunks. Addie's was to be starboard and forward, one of two cabins on either side of the forward passage. The other would be Kit's. Jean Claude explained that most 70-foot sloops would not have such spacious forward berths, but because of the Bruce King design's wide beam, Kit and Addie would be most comfortable, tucked away on opposite sides of the passageway. Jim drew the most forward cabin in the bow. Jean Claude agreed to share the very large captain's aft cabin with Ian, since they would be on opposite shifts and each could sleep when the other was on watch. Ian explained that they would install a lee cloth in the center of the berth to hold them in place while they slept on the low side under heel.

All settled in, Addie began to notice the finer details of the pristine sailing vessel. The interior was covered in handcrafted cherry and mahogany cabinetry, walls and floors throughout. The fabrics on the cushions were a plush and luxurious dark blue with fine, beige trim cording around the edges. The flawlessly varnished splendor, both inside and out, hinted of its owner's extreme care. Addie wondered if Ian owned the *True Tilt* as well as serving as her Captain. At the right moment, she would ask him.

All provisioned and packed away, they were ready to sail ahead of schedule. Ian doled out doses of Sturgeron, a preventive med for seasickness, "To get everyone through the first leg." Each of them had been assigned shifts at the helm, three hours on, three hours off. Kit, Jim and Addie would be paired with either Ian or Jean Claude for the first day, until they had their sea legs and understood their responsibilities more. Jim focused on the charts at the nav station with Jean Claude and studied the screens in front of him, pushing buttons and moving the cursor to program the waypoints and final destination. Ian listened to the weather report and checked the wind direction against what he'd heard earlier in the day. The wind had clocked around more to the west, so he made adjustments to his plan. He barked an order at Kit and Addie, to go over to the marina and report that they'd depart on time.

The two women climbed up the companionway, jumped over the side of the boat, and walked down the long dock until they ran into what appeared to be a local dockhand wearing the familiar Tilt polo. His ebony skin shone brightly in the hot tropical sun. His matted dreadlocks were bound in a big nest on the back of his head and he spoke in a rich, singsong, Island Carib voice. Brow furrowed, he stopped to give the "ladies" some instructions for the voyage.

"Ya best be pick up yer foot and run, now that the rain is held up, ta be sure. Go long yer way, mon! Yes, be long with yerself. Don wan yer luck to run out, now do ya? All de decks are clean and de Capn' be impatient fer ya to provision and go! Don be a fool-fool and get on outta here NOW will ya? Tell Cap'n Ian, time ta go!"

Wondering why he seemed worried, Addie inquired to satisfy her curiosity, but also to address a lurking fear. "Is there a rush to get moving for some reason?" She noticed Kit's intense focus on the man, as if she was picking up on something, too.

"Oh yes, mon. The luck of da sea can be fickle and ye best be on wid yerself. That Cap'n Ian, he has a hard ear sometime. If ya nuh cater ta da chores well, den ya gonna be trouble. Uh huh. Truss me. Less ya wanna be on dat bamsee whole night da furst nite? Get on now and go!" He waved his big black arm with great fanfare, shooing them off to leave.

Looking sideways at Kit, Addie almost exploded in laughter but kept her wits about her. "What in the world was he talking about, Kit?"

"Jean Claude told me his nickname is 'Ole Yoda Bam Bam.' He has some kind of sixth sense and everyone down in Road Town comes to him for advice. He seems to have a talent for predicting trouble or something." Kit's eyebrows raised enough to betray her concern.

In the distance, Ole Yoda appeared to be talking loudly to himself. "Dem gyals both de glamma gyals. Better tell dat Ian to treat em tops and not be no sweet mon! No sirree." And he scurried off around the corner.

Kit signed out the *True Tilt* at the dispatcher office, then she and Addie stopped by the marina provision store to address Ian's last request. They picked up four bags of crushed ice and headed back to the yacht. An eerie feeling settled in Addie's stomach as she acknowledged there was no turning back now. Back on-board, she began to feel queasy in anticipation of the motion.

Tossing off the permanent lines to a nearby dockhand, Ian drew the remaining lines onto the boat. Jean Claude showed everyone how to properly coil the lines and stow them safely in the deck lockers, then pulled in the fenders and stowed them as well. Addie found a strange pleasure in observing the deck duties being performed by the methodical Jean Claude. Very organized, decisive and precise. *Sailing just might agree with me after all.*

Ian fired up the motor and whistled loudly. A loud, even, bumping sound from behind was approaching closer, when out of the blue a brown and white, furry animal jumped onto deck.

"Ahoy, mate, welcome aboard!" shouted Ian at the beatnik-looking dog. "Where've you been, you scoundrel, out chasing the gyals again?" He smiled broadly, with obvious affection.

"Is he yours?" Jim asked. "What kind of hound is that anyway?"

"He's a Portuguese Water Dog. Barnacle's his name. Sticks to my side like a barnacle on a piling, unless he's out prowling for female types." Ian laughed. The shaggy dog pranced right up to the bow and out onto the bowsprit, angling his body between the bars for a perfect guard-dog spot right out front. "He likes to be on watch, so he can see the fish first!"

Everything and everyone on-board now, they were ready to depart. As they motored out of Soper's Hole and rounded the north side of the island to head out of the channel, the wind picked up and Jean Claude motioned to Kit to help raise the sails. Feeling nervous because the motion of the waves was picking up, but more afraid of looking like a chicken, Addie went forward with them and asked how she could help. Handing her the winch handle, J.C. positioned the hardware and prepared to hoist the mainsail. Taking back the handle, he placed it into the winch and began turning the crank. After showing Kit how it was done, he turned the job over to her, mentioning that Addie should watch to learn as well. It was harder than it looked, but Kit managed to wedge herself into the safety of the granny bars and rotated the handle until the sail caught wind and finished its own ascent without the need for any muscle. Tying off the lines, J.C. neatened up the extras and headed back to the cockpit.

Nerves taut, all Addie wanted right now was to sit down and concentrate on holding her wits together. It was taking a certain amount of mind control to keep herself from panicking. She had to admit, though, it was a beautiful day and it promised to be a lovely experience. *So far, so good.*

Once the sails were in place and the southbound course set for a waypoint just west of St. Croix, Ian called everyone together for a lesson on the ship's rules and the plan of action for emergency situations. This included a trip below into the engine room to learn how to troubleshoot engine, battery power and water maker problems. This was territory Addie knew a little bit about, since she ran hotels and had similar risk management plans. She knew what to do with her surroundings, particularly when risk was imminent. Problem-solving was one of her gifts. It kept her mind off of the *other fear* just beneath the surface. She figured when she learned more about the world of sailing, she'd be able to troubleshoot. This appealed to the "safety girl" in her who liked contingency planning.

Just then a loud thump knocked on the side of the vessel. Seeing the surprise on Ian's face contributed to their curiosity. Everyone scurried up the companionway above deck. Barnacle was excited and jumping around in circles. Ian looked around for clues as everyone watched in silence. All of a sudden, a large dolphin jumped out of the surf and chattered loudly, trying to get their attention.

"Oh, its YOU, Lucy!" exclaimed Ian.

Jean Claude laughed with delight as he slowed down the engine. Ian leaned over the transom at the rear of the cockpit. Just then, Lucy jumped again and flipped a 360-degree turn in mid-air before diving back into the water.

"She's come to escort us out to sea," said Ian. "Lucy is a trained dolphin brought here by her trainer when they were filming a movie years ago. When it was time to go, they couldn't find her and had to leave her behind. She hangs out around Cane Garden Bay on the other side of the island most of the time. She loves to swim with the cruising sailors and will let you stroke her if she gets to know you. She's quite the famous girl around here, eh Jean Claude? And a pal of Barnacle's, too. " He winked. "She even has her own family now, including a baby of her own."

"Indeed, she was here last time I was here and that was quite a while ago," Jean Claude chimed in. "She sure knows her boats. Must have wanted to come hitch a ride out with us in our draft. She does love those fast sailors!" Jean Claude and Ian reminisced about a dive adventure they'd had with Lucy on the last trip. She'd been a good companion and helped them find their way back to the boat when their drift dive had carried them too far away. Barnacle kept running to the lifeline gate and barking, obviously wanting to jump in and swim with Lucy.

"Not this time, boy," chided Ian. "We've got a long haul ahead of us and we must be away with ourselves!" Barnacle sat down and cocked his head to the side, as if he understood what Ian was saying. Then he sighed heavily with a loud "Humph!"

What a funny dog, Addie thought. *Like a teenager, when his dad says no he can't do something. He's just about human.* This journey was starting out well. She loved animals, and especially sea life. She'd been resort SCUBA diving several times and was on Barnacle's side, wishing they'd stop and she could dive in and play with Lucy. She forgot all about the motion of the boat around her and started to relax into the quest.

Chapter 11

The sailing lessons of the day were complete, all the sails were up, and the crew had successfully rounded east of St. Croix, heading due south to the Windward Islands. Their next stop was to be an island in St. Pierre called Martinique, originally settled by the French. Ian projected three full days of sailing to make it to port in time to check in and get some provisions. The shifts at the helm were mapped out on a clipboard and everyone had been taught how to record their hourly data check-in on the chart. Longitude and latitude, as well as wind direction, course headings, boat speed and water traffic noted along the way, were all items to be neatly recorded so the navigator could report the journey's progress to the Captain.

Aside from operating the helm and keeping the vessel on course, the other important duty when at the helm (besides trying not to vomit) was to turn one's head 180 degrees both ways every five minutes to check for traffic. Ian said they had to be on the defensive because ships at higher speeds could fail to notice them, and be on top of them in minutes. He told dramatic stories about sailboats sawed in half by larger vessels, drowning entire cruising families aboard. Alertness was key. This was why he was so strict about taking shifts no longer than three hours and getting sleep in between.

Keeping her mind occupied learning tasks and duties had done its trick for Addie. The waves didn't seem that big, so she was beginning to relax and feeling only a little queasy. The balmy afternoon breeze had turned into a swift, crisp wind from behind, the boat careening along easily with the motion. Everyone was relaxing around the cockpit and enjoying a bit of leisurely conversation while the sky turned pink and the sun began its downward traverse.

Barnacle snuggled up next to Addie in her corner of the cockpit where she'd wrapped her legs with a small boat blanket.

Kit went below to serve up the dinner Jean Claude had prepared and placed in the oven earlier. She was full of energy, chattering up the companionway and joining in the conversation as she served up plates, claiming she loved to be busy. Jean Claude had reluctantly given in to her, pulling out his expensive-looking camera and trying to catch the sunset at just the right time.

"So, Ian, who are all of these strange people we keep meeting with weird names?" Jim asked, as if reading Addie's mind.

"Oh, you mean the Guides?" Ian responded as if this were something everyone should know.

"The Guides?" Jim asked.

"Yeah, the Guides you meet along the way in life. It simply tells me you must have been listening. You know, many people we run into as we go through life may be messengers for our journey, people who have something to teach us. Those are the Guides. Or they might be the Mirrors or the Tempters. Trick is to know the difference and to pick up on what you need to learn just then."

Jim wasn't quite buying this line of thought. "Well, I've been alive a long time and I daresay I've never met any 'Guides' before now. At least not with names so explicit to the situation."

"As I said, it tells me you've started listening. The Guides have always been there, but you might not have been paying attention. When you become a Seeker, you start listening and seeing differently."

There's that word again, thought Addie. *Seeker.*

"What he's saying is true," agreed Jean Claude. "That's what started happening to me on my first trip here. But it was only because of what I'd gone through and how it changed me, when I was ready to face the fact that I needed to go on living. Everyone has these choice points, but I didn't think I was going to recover from mine."

"Choice point? What was it, do you mind telling us?" Jim was curious because of the experience that had turned *him* inside out.

"I lost my wife five years ago in a dive accident. I stopped caring if I lived or died for a while. I don't know how I chose life, but what saved me was signing up for a grueling challenge called the Whitbread race. I focused on the around-the-world challenge and our captain led me out of the darkness with his great sense of wisdom. That's when the Guides started showing up, to give me hope or to show me something important about myself. Or maybe I had to choose life before I could start noticing them, I can't remember now." Jean Claude's admission was a tender moment and everyone fell silent for a while.

Except Barnacle, who raised his head to get Addie's attention. She'd stopped rubbing it for a moment, thinking it wasn't exactly a soft experience to be petting the wiry-headed goofball with mats under his curly coat. *He needs a bath. Has shrimp-breath, too. I'll have to talk with Ian about grooming him better.*

Kit's head emerged from the galley and she started passing bowls of seafood pasta up to the others. "I was listening to you, Jean Claude, and I have to tell you I had a tough loss of my own recently. Not like yours, but it threw me into a place where I don't want to be. My brother died in a plane crash a year ago. Especially when I'm alone, my mind turns to memories of him. We were very close and I haven't been doing very well. I used to be so certain about everything and then my world was turned upside down. Can't say I've gotten it back together, either." Obviously embarrassed about her own admission, Kit changed the subject. "Now, chow down, cuz I've been slaving away down here in the heat and I'm dying to get up there and get some air!"

"Come on up Kit, I'll clean up the rest after dinner," Addie said. She suddenly felt empathy for the strong and capable Kit. She knew personally why Kit was making light of her pain. She'd done that for years herself.

"It seems we've all had some wake-up calls lately," Jim added, looking around and then directly at Addie as if asking her to share. She nodded her head in agreement, but was not ready to put words to what she was feeling.

Ian nodded at Jean Claude in thanks for sharing his story. This was J.C.'s second time on this trip. His loss had been so great, he'd not been able to regain his purpose fully the first time. Ian was glad he was back. He had so much to offer. "So," Ian said, "I hope you're all starting to see we have some things in common with each other on this trip. It's an important mission for all of us. When an epiphany or choice point shows up, it's a sign that life is shaping us and preparing us for our destiny. To give the gift that only we can give, that we are uniquely created to offer to others. Life includes tragedy, crisis and opportunity; but some care only about getting back to equilibrium instead of growing from the experience. They never get beyond a certain level of creative contribution, because they prefer a head-in-the-sand approach to survival. But some become Seekers. They take on the challenge of using their suffering to become stronger, more caring individuals who contribute to the good of humanity in big ways. Facing a choice point with courage and insight turns us into who we were meant to be. The path we choose after a life crisis matters. The divide can be wide, indeed, between those who continue to take from the world and those who evolve to give back in meaningful ways."

The sky spilled forth in a rainbow of orange and gray and the waves from behind the stern rocked the *True Tilt* gently from side to side. As Jean Claude captured luminous photo after photo, the crew slipped quietly into the arms of nature's great rocking chair. Soothing and rhythmic, the sea was their healer. Five souls coming together on a journey. Disparate stories. And yet strikingly *all the same.*

Chapter 12

In the basement of the Paramount Hotel in Miami, Nicolai called a meeting. With this small group of disgruntled misfits, he was certain he could contain the secrecy required to succeed at his plan. He'd made up names so he could think of them as pawns instead of people. *The Hacker* had been indicted for embezzlement. The large, fleshy man he called *Brutus,* with tattoos all over his exposed flesh and a perpetual frown, hadn't been exactly easy to hire, but the company's diversity policy had helped Nicolai there. Brutus would be perfect for the dirty work that was beneath Nicolai. He'd told the misfits they would each get a large bonus for the project.

The third member of the clandestine team was a small, quiet, sharp-eyed Asian woman he called *Nono.* A Chinese mother and American father had smuggled her to the States after she was born, and she spoke several dialects of Chinese. Knowing her papers were forged, Nicolai felt certain Nono would do anything he told her. She needed the money to take care of her aging parents and wasn't aware of the plan's details. He wanted someone who wouldn't ask questions to manage all communication with the others. He himself would not be involved. If everything went according to plan, he would not be a suspect. He would simply announce he was leaving the company to buy a hotel in Trinidad.

Nicolai smiled as he thought how shocked they'd be that he had the means to pull off such a transaction. His colleagues upstairs would have underestimated him yet again. He had plans for himself that did not include rotting in this slow-moving company. Not twice, but three times, he'd been turned down for a promotion. He relished the thought of their regret when he pocketed the profits from the takeover transaction. By the time they found the money was gone, he would already be back in Trinidad enjoying his wealth and power.

The dirty basement office where they met, previously occupied by security and now unused, had meager furniture and supplies. Nicolai didn't care about the contrast to the fine furnishings in the top floor suites where his enemies gloated from their corner offices. He should have been there, but they weren't smart enough to include him. He'd spent years upon years programming the systems now used by everyone in the company. A flush of anger spread through his body as he recalled his last rejection from the CEO of the Caribbean-based hotel division, who took barely five minutes to tell him he wouldn't be getting the promotion to CTO. Instead, they brought in some highbrow graduate of an Ivy League School. This was the blow that would change his life forever. And theirs. He'd make sure of that. He'd gone over their heads and made a deal with the man who would soon take over the chain. They'd soon regret not recognizing how intelligent he was. When people underestimated him, it made him furious. But he would get even soon enough.

The Hacker would get him into the banking system, and as soon as the money came in from the transaction, he'd transfer it and head for the airport. He'd hired someone to get rid of the two co-conspirators left behind so he wouldn't have to worry about them ratting on him later. He had other plans for Brutus. He was certain he had control of them until the plan was carried out, because he knew their secrets. More importantly, he'd tested them to prove they could be bought.

Nicolai had fooled them all into thinking this was a company project and would make sure each one of them knew the risk of spoiling his plans. He'd learned his acting skills very early in life, pretending to be okay when his stepfather was doing unspeakable things to him behind his mother's back. He was good at giving people what they wanted, to secure his own freedom. Those skills would come in handy now.

Nicolai's plan was about to unfold. He had to make one more trip to the lower Caribbean, and then all the parts would be in place. The Viking was a fast powerboat and he could catch up with his prey in less than two days.

Once he had them out of the way, he would have everything he'd dreamed of for so many years. They would not get their hands on that treasure. It should have belonged to his family and he intended to take what was his. It was his destiny. He'd known it since he found the letter. His father had been a coward, but he would not be.

Chapter 13

It was the midnight watch, and Addie wasn't used to so much quiet. The sea made a long, low, swooshing sound every few minutes as it folded itself around the hull between large waves. Wind whistled lightly in the sails, the only other sound an occasional thump when the sail strained and slapped back against the restriction of the mast lines.

J.C. quietly busied himself with the chartplotter and radar. Two hours had gone by and the two of them had said only a few words, so Addie let her thoughts drift astray and generally observed her surroundings. So far, she'd felt fairly well, so she was in good spirits and taking in the black sky full of millions of stars. *Why doesn't the sky look like this in the city? It's magnificent, lit up like a Christmas tree!* The ocean gave the appearance of a large black plastic bag undulating with something alive within, and she shivered at the thought of what lay beneath the huge body of water.

Addie had recently read, in a *Cruising World* magazine Ian had left in the parlor, that one of the greatest dangers at sea was running into a sleeping whale. *Yet another thing to obsess about.* She looked back at the sky to inspire her to think of much bigger things.

Savoring the quiet and needing the time to reflect, Addie was enjoying the company of a man who apparently needed the same. They both busied themselves with their duties and before long the three-hour watch was complete. Addie recorded the stats on the clipboard and yawned as she slipped off her tether and headed below for a six-hour nap before her 9 a.m. watch.

J.C. smiled, appreciating that Addie had let the time go by without trivial conversation. He guessed she was in awe of being at sea for the first time. He didn't know she was left wordless because she was so awed by his company.

Relieved to say her goodnights, Addie tagged in Kit and Ian for the next shift and hit her cabin to crash in the arms of the steady rocking motion. She felt the lovely exhaustion of a day full of physical tasks and, breathing a sigh of relief, acknowledged how good it was to be in the middle of nothing but nature. The smells, sights and sounds were so compelling they drew her away from the head full of problems that usually prevented falling asleep. *I could get used to this.* She pushed away thoughts about the acquisition and what might be going on back at Stanton Suites and Pyramid, deciding there would be plenty of time later to worry about what was happening to her great little company. *A mind cleared of clutter is a mind that can give in to deep, sound sleep.* And sleep she did. For the first time in months.

Chapter 14

Kit had finished her shift at 9 a.m. when she pulled Addie aside during the shift change and asked her to come into her cabin for a minute. Surprised at the mess everything was in, Addie asked her what was going on. Giving a side glance to the mess, Kit brushed it aside with a wave of her hand. "Not that. I just wanted to ask you what you think about the treasure map. I couldn't sleep all night! I kept dreaming about jewels and coins and the excitement of adventure! Do you think we've been brought on this voyage to find it? I spoke to Jim about it, and he thinks so, too. After all, he was the one given the map. Did you see the mark on the map is an island just south of St. Vincent? Ian said we're headed there. I think we've been brought together to solve this puzzle and we're going to be rewarded for it if we take control of the situation and go for it. But we have to have our act together, figure out if Ian and Jean Claude know anything about it. Did you find out anything from him on your shift last night?"

At this early hour, Addie could hardly keep up with the words tumbling from Kit's mouth. "Well, you may be right, but I say we should wait to see what unfolds. We need to be cautious and not jump to conclusions. Ian seems to know what's going on and why we're here. He hasn't mentioned any treasure. Maybe Jim getting that map was a coincidence and doesn't have anything to do with our task here."

"But look at this!" Kit pointed to the map. "The big red crossbones marking on this map is right on Mayreau, and I saw Ian entering our final destination into the chart plotter yesterday. It's MAYREAU. That can't be a coincidence!"

Addie conceded that Kit might have a point. Many things seemed like coincidences lately and all of them appeared to lead to this particular path.

"We need a strategy," Kit insisted. "We might know something even Ian doesn't know! What if he's not exactly sure why we're here and thinks it's about something else? I think we have to at least have a strategy for checking it out when we get there."

A knock on the door interrupted her diatribe and gave Addie a few moments to ponder.

"Yes?" Kit asked.

"You two all right in there?" It was Jean Claude. "Addie, you're up on deck next and you're late."

"Sure we're just fine! Be out in a minute."

"Well, breakfast is served. Western omelets with fresh mango salsa and a pot of strong breakfast tea to open your eyes. Come on now."

I could get used to this guy, Addie thought. *There's a creative aspect in his being so well rounded. A real Renaissance man. Plus, something about his demeanor has made me begin to trust him. And I don't trust easily.*

Satisfied that she'd gotten Addie's attention, Kit said her good nights after breakfast and headed to her cabin for some shuteye to make up for the three hours she lost during the night shift. Addie gobbled up her omelet in record time, carrying her tea up to the helm to manage the 9 - noon day shift.

Jim and Jean Claude were busy talking about the headings and weather report at the nav station while Addie breathed in the beauty and peace of the morning sky. It was calm and the wind was light. A huge multi-colored sail billowed out from the front of the boat. The angular patterns of the sailcloth spilled out into concentric circles of red, orange, yellow and green. Jean Claude had explained this was a spinnaker sail and had replaced the genoa, which had been there the night before. This kind of sail was better for this morning's light air. Though more fragile than the genoa, the spinnaker was much larger and could catch a lot more wind. "The tougher genoa was good for catching the fifteen to twenty knots of strong wind we had yesterday," he said, "but today we have only eight knots from behind us."

Addie liked the slower pace and lovely palette of color. The wonders of sailing were beginning to open her land-locked emotions. Practicing the helmsman duties captured her thoughts and she focused on the rhythm of the waves and wind, balancing the response of the helm in her hands as it spun back and forth. The *True Tilt* seemed to almost sail herself when you got her into what Ian called the "true tilt" for the conditions. *She speaks to her helmsman as a lover does, guiding the helmsman's hand where she wants it to go.* The balance of it all was fascinating to Addie: the telltales, little six-inch threads half way up the mainsail that lined themselves parallel to the horizon when they liked the exact amount of wind in them; the instruments that showed how to keep the bow in the right direction, but not at the sacrifice of the best position for maximum wind optimization. Precise, yet not precise. Balanced, yet tilted. Everything in place to capture the optimum capacity possible from the given conditions. But different every time. The trim of the sails depended entirely on gauging environmental conditions before finding the sweet spot – the exact "true tilt" for the current situation.

It struck her that the principles of sailing were a lot like life. *One never knows where the currents might threaten to take you, but you can check the wind direction, its presenting velocity, and work with it while coaxing the vessel in the general direction of your destination. All of it in balance, and you at the helm. Guiding, but knowing the universe is bigger than you are, so you can't possibly control what unfolds. Unpredictable storms may take you off course. But you can adjust your sails, point to the next waypoint, and still arrive there in the end.* Hours went by as she ruminated about the metaphor of the sea to life. Then she suddenly became alert, aware of changes.

The wind smelled slightly different than it had yesterday. The air had grown heavier and the spinnaker had started to flop and sag, almost complaining to her. Addie noted on the clipboard the ominous-looking yacht that had been following their path for the entire shift. Through the binoculars she saw the vessel was an austere-appearing powerboat with black windows that looked like eyes, still too far away to make out any details. Now it appeared on the radar screen, too, so she made a notation that it was within the *True Tilt's* radar range and should be watched on the next shift. Wondering if she should alert someone, Addie looked 180 degrees around again. Something about the vessel gave her the creeps.

Jean Claude was busy at the nav station and Ian had gotten up to join him. They were talking excitedly about something. Addie finished up the paperwork and greeted Jim, who seemed tired as he climbed up the companionway, with dark bags under his eyes. So far he'd been such a cheerful sort, and this seemed out of character. When Addie handed him a cup of hot steaming tea and a plate of food, he smiled in puppy-dog-like gratitude, endearing for such a big guy. Barnacle seemed to sense Jim's mood and plopped down next to him as he ate his lunch before taking over for Addie at noon.

"Hey there, ole licorice lips. You just want my food don't you?" Jim chuckled.

"Yeah, you've got his number," said Addie, "Tossed him a scrap yesterday and almost pulled back a stub. I swear he's got a long row of teeth that snap as quick as a gator."

Addie finished off her last few watch duties, listening as Jean Claude accepted the order from Ian to change out the sails. He said he'd be up in a moment to assist. Addie decided not to say anything about the creepy yacht. This was just one of numerous vessels she'd recorded over the last twenty-four hours. As she went forward to her cabin, she heard Ian say, "There goes our weather window. That damned wind has clocked around again."

PART THREE

THE HEROES

Courage ~ **The call of justice gives rise to integrity, and the Warrior becomes the Hero.**

"Great injustices and human vulnerability are the elixir that calls the Hero to action."

- Pam Boney

Chapter 15

Kit was at the helm and intently focused on the task at hand. The winds whistled through the halyards and banged them against the mast with intermittent thuds. They were still at full sail, with the stronger genoa replacing the fragile spinnaker. The waves were growing bigger by the minute, crashing against the bow, sending salty sprays of water onto the forward deck. Lightning pierced the sky at a distance, and loud claps of thunder seemed right above them, though Ian assured everyone the storm was still a mile or two away. At his crisp order, the hatches and portals had been closed tight and loose items in the cabins stowed away. His confidence in this volatile situation was impressive. He was alert and curt in his communication.

Kit, Jim and Ian were all topside now, while Jean Claude snored away in the aft berth.

Ian had suggested Addie try to sleep so she could be fresh for the next shift, but sleep was not going to happen for her. The waves crashing against the bow reverberated through the hollows of the cabin and her head pounded in unison, as if her brain was trying to fight back. Yawning over and over and feeling her fatigue did not provide enough physical distraction to overcome the annoying, fearful thoughts that kept her from sleep. Those and, of course, her stomach. The washing machine motion of the vessel was unpredictable, and Ian had told her to keep her eyes closed when below to ward off one of the many triggers of seasickness. He'd explained that the eyes receiving confusing signals from excessive motion triggers an emitter response of fear. This sets into motion a line of defense that's part of the human design for survival. When the mind thinks there's danger, it knows to prepare the body for fight or flight, both of which require the majority of blood flow to other parts of the body than the stomach. Thus it quickly generates a command to the stomach to empty its contents, so that precious blood supply can be rerouted to the main torso and legs. It's a matter of priority. Survival 101, involuntary style!

All of this made wonderful sense and helped Addie manage her thoughts fairly well in good weather. But her fears seemed to hijack her ability to access logic now that danger signs were apparent and her thoughts had quickly started going south. She was in a strange place, with strangers, on a mysterious mission, with the prospect of heavy weather. Now that they were well underway, and getting OFF of the boat was no longer an option, all of this was also entirely unavoidable. Addie's "in control, self-preserving instincts" did not like this scenario and its shortage of good alternatives. It appeared she was quite stuck and without an escape plan! Add this peril to her paranoid concerns about the austere-looking boat following them, and things were not adding up very nicely for her orderly preferences. She felt like a rock was sitting in her increasingly heavy stomach. A cold sweat peppered her brow and upper chest. She needed to get to the bathroom, but didn't dare move for fear of losing any semblance of control and composure. Frustrated and exhausted, Addie was also worried she was getting nowhere in her duty to prepare for the next watch by getting some rest. She was obsessing about a drink of water when Ian looked in to check on her.

He immediately saw her condition. "Up you go now, get some air. It's pretty rough down here and not a good place to be in a storm if you're not used to it. Put your foulies on, take this Sturgeron tablet, grab your water jug and come on up into the cockpit with the rest of us. Jean Claude can get some sleep and take charge later. And close your eyes. That can limit the danger signal to your brain."

As soon as Addie stood up, she felt an involuntary surge from her gut and Ian quickly pushed her around the corner and into the head. Coming back out, Addie realized she'd lost all concern about what anyone thought about her. The relief she felt after unloading her stomach was exhilarating. Brushing her teeth and pulling her foulies out of the locker, she squeezed her eyes closed and felt her way along the companionway as she climbed up top.

Much to her amazement, the fresh air was a welcome reprieve, in spite of the storm. The foreboding feeling she'd felt earlier was replaced with a sliver of hope. Addie tried to smile at her companions, though it was forced. *Am I the only ninny who feels so bad I can barely breathe?* Remembering Jim's face from earlier, she was a little comforted that a big strong guy could be seasick, too. Most of the time she hated being "a girl" and felt she should be able to hang with the guys. She was glad to be in company with Jim, who could hold his own in most situations but was just as intimidated as she was in this new arena of challenge. She didn't want "wimpy" to be associated with "woman."

Unlike Addie and Jim, Kit looked fabulous and in her element. Her forehead was knit with pure physical will. In her red and white protective foulies, and very much in charge, she looked like an old pro at the helm of the great vessel. It was obvious she was having a fabulous time. The waves had grown so large they were crashing over the bow, spilling around the windshield protecting the cockpit and onto the sides of the teak deck. Small rivers of water were forming all around the deck and disappearing into the scuppers, taking the water back out to sea. About every fourth or fifth wave was bigger than the others and water would spray right into Kit's face, making her laugh out loud. She was using her sunglasses as a windshield and enjoying the splash as if it were some kind of whitewater rafting extravaganza. Her wild red mane was tucked inside the hood of the jacket, so she was fully covered and reveling in the exchange with nature. Kit hollered over the noise of the wind, "How utterly exhilarating it is to have this great vessel in my hands and to know Mother Nature is trying to beat me!"

"And you have no intention of losing, that's clear!" said Jim, laughing out loud. "You're just plain crazy, that's the deal with you!" But his face was pale and tired beneath his weak grin.

"I wish I could be having that much fun." Addie said this in her most pathetic victim voice. She really didn't like the girl in her who withdrew too easily from challenging settings. Give her a balance sheet and a problem to analyze, and she was in her zone. *That's why I hate vacations. I love to be adventurous on vacations but I'm not "all in" because of the fear. My inner conflict is grueling and exhausting.*

Ian had gone forward to "reef" the genoa – bring it down a bit to reduce the wind catch – when suddenly a blast of wind hit and was countered by a wave pushing in the opposite direction. The boat lurched, forcing the crew over so far to starboard, Ian was thrown off of his feet, landing with force against the forward stanchions, flipping over the side and disappearing into the water.

A scream pummeled from Addie's throat. Kit yelled to Jim to go wake up Jean Claude, but before Jim could even move, Jean Claude flew up the companionway, popping his tether into place and moving up to the bow in the flash of a few seconds. Addie jumped up and stepped over the side of the cockpit and onto the deck to peer over the side. Ian was hanging on by the tether that had locked him to the safety jacklines on deck. Kneeling down, she could hold her balance while keeping her eyes on him. Her head was pounding and she was in problem-solving mode. *What should we do first, what are the physics of this situation, how is he attached, how long can he last like that, what do we have to work with?*

Ian's body banged against the side of the boat and was dragged under with every wave. To keep from being knocked out he struggled against the pressure of the water, holding onto the tether line with his right hand, while attempting to hold his body away from the side of the boat with his left hand. Every now and then he surfaced to grab a big breath, and a mountainous wave would pull him under again.

Addie was terrified by the sound of the slamming and seeing the big strong man being pulled beneath the surface like a fish on the hook.

Jean Claude had crawled to the forward deck and hollered back to Jim to grab the Man Overboard Life Preserver off the aft stanchion. They'd practiced a man-overboard exercise on day one, but this wasn't going according to plan. Jean Claude fastened a line holding the preserver to the mid-ship cleat and tossed it over to Ian, just missing his bobbing head. Ian's arms thrashed about, trying to grab the preserver, but it was tied too far behind him. J.C. pulled it back in and this time threw it in front of Ian, who caught it with his left hand and struggled to pull his body, now heavy with waterlogged clothes, onto the life preserver. The wind howled, unabated.

This is just the first step, thought Addie. Knowing the real challenge was going to be getting Ian up and over the side of the boat, she madly thought of solutions. *We have his head above water but he won't last long like that. I read something about that in the instruction book I was studying. What was it? Never mind, just think of the physics. How do we get him back over that daunting distance from the waterline to the boat? It has to be at least five or six feet to the toe-rail and the power of the water is dragging him down. The boat is bouncing in large leaps between waves and providing, at best, an unpredictable platform to work from. We need something to leverage our strength! Or, we need to slow down! That's it! We need to stop if we can.*

Remembering the lessons Ian had given them their first day on-board, Addie looked around at the controls of the boat. The engine was off. This would mean, she remembered, they were being propelled by the sails as their source of power. Ian had been trying to lower them when he was knocked overboard. What did he call it, reefing the sails? *That's it; we need to pull them back in to slow down. Tell Jean Claude to save his strength for a better set of circumstances. We have to get the sails down first.*

Just then, Jean Claude yelled "Fall off! Fall Off! Now!" and looked at Kit, his furrowed brow showing his concern that she hadn't already had the sense to fall off. Kit seemed confused for a moment and looked at Addie.

Addie realized she was the only one who'd studied their sailing terms homework. *Fall off? What does that mean?* She didn't know what the words meant exactly, but she understood the general principle of physics that was happening under sail. "Kit, I think it means turn away from the wind so it falls out of the sails!"

"Okay, steer away from the wind. You got it." Kit said.

Addie was glad Kit knew which way the wind was, because THAT she did not know. She made a mental note to find out how to do that later. *Decent teamwork, putting our skills together, but we each had missing pieces, which was not a good thing.*

As Kit turned the *True Tilt* away from the wind, the boat began to slow, though it still rocked chaotically in the waves. This gave them enough pause to think about what to do next. Jean Claude was trying to pull Ian in by the tether again and it wasn't working. The force of the water moving against Ian's body was still too strong to work against.

"I have an idea," Jim said. "What if we get some lines around Ian and pull him closer to the boat? Maybe we can roll him up sideways."

"I don't see how we can get them around him without his help," said Jean Claude, "Jim, what other ideas do you have?"

"Let me go look around in the lockers and see if I can find anything that will help." Jim disappeared into the cabin.

The sails had begun to flap around wildly, making disconcertingly loud banging noises. The forward sail was loose now and J.C. suddenly yelled an order to shorten sail, genoa first.

Looking at Addie for direction again, Kit seemed puzzled and almost angry. Addie grabbed the winch handle. Thinking carefully about which side should pull in the genoa, she placed the handle into the winch and wrapped the furling line around the drum the way she'd observed J.C. doing it before. Once it was secure, she started cranking the handle and pulling in the sail.

Just then Jim came above deck and saw the mainsail flapping, so he tightened it by pulling the mainsheet. He looked deflated as he told Jean Claude all he could find was the boat hook, and his best idea was to loop the line over the boat hook and stretch it out over Ian to extend a lasso hoop around him somewhere. The boat bounced up and down like an angry two-year-old, waves crashing on deck, but at least the sails were now secured and not flapping around dangerously, as they had been moments before. Jim extended the boat hook over Ian's legs, waiting for him to raise his feet so Jim could lasso the lower half of his body. Ian understood. With tremendous strain, he tried three times to thrust his feet together in the air by leveraging the preserver under his heavier upper torso. On the third try, Jim was able to get the lasso around both feet and pulled tightly to get leverage. Then he and Jean Claude pressed their feet against the toe-rail for balance and, holding onto both ends of the lines, pulled with all their strength. Ian had just been pummeled by a large wave and gasped for air. His pale skin even paler, he looked almost listless. His right hand was bleeding badly and a red cloud of blood expanded in the water around it.

As they managed to get him halfway to the boat, a huge wave crashed into their backs and both men lost their grip. Ian fell back into the water with a splash, this time limited with no legs to use because they were tied together. Almost a split second later, they all heard another big splash behind them. Kit yelled, "That stupid dog has jumped into the water!" Barnacle swam with determination toward the bow to save his master.

"Mon Dieu," yelled Jean Claude, "someone call him back! Call him back now! He's only going to make things worse!"

Kit and Addie both called Barnacle frantically. The boat was not moving forward but was heaving to in the wild waves, and it had begun to rain harder, substantially reducing visibility.

Out of the corner of her eye, Addie noticed something else moving in the water twenty yards away. Something big. The slick gray skin of the large creature grew larger as it came closer and a fin popped up above the surface as the big wave subsided. A shark, a very large shark, was interested in what was going on. Barnacle had closed the distance between him and his master, now almost right behind Ian.

Terror rose from Addie's gut and she screamed bloody murder.

Kit yelled at Addie to get her head together and shoved her in front of the helm, ordering her to take the wheel. Before anyone could figure out what she was doing, Kit stripped off her foulies and dove straight over the lifeline at the side of the boat, headed toward Barnacle.

Addie froze in terror as she watched the scene unfold. The fin was approaching again, rolling in the waves and then disappearing. It was less than ten feet from Barnacle when it veered off in the opposite direction and disappeared. Kit reached Barnacle, threw her arms over the dog's upper torso and under his front legs in a powerful grip and started swimming back toward the ladder she'd seen at the base of the transom behind the cockpit.

Jean Claude yelled to Addie to drop the ladder for a swift escape.

Addie couldn't tear her eyes away from the water. She knew sharks could smell a drop of blood from miles away and Ian's struggle below, coupled with the splashing of a dog, made a particularly attractive scene for dinner. She also knew sharks investigate with a couple of rounds, bumping their potential prey to test it and then going in for the kill, a move that's swift, powerful and almost always deadly. The pressure from the jaws of a large shark can crush bones and rip body parts off like people tearing tender chicken off a bone. Addie, a zealot about watching the *Discovery Channel,* was especially obsessed about anything to do with avoiding danger. Self-preservation held keen interest for her. She stared at the water and prayed silently that Kit was fast enough to get the dog and herself out of the water before the shark returned. She dropped the ladder and held her breath for what seemed a long time.

Jean Claude was trying to hoist Ian up again on his own but was clearly straining to hold onto the single tether. Jim had a couple of dock lines rigged along the side of the boat now and as J.C. pulled Ian closer, Jim was able to get a handle on the lasso around his foot again as it pivoted up from a wave. The two of them pulled Ian's body close to the side of the boat, using both ends to bring him sideways against the hull. Now that the boat had slowed down, this provided a safer scenario and seemed less likely to knock him out. Just then Jim saw the shark approaching Ian, and Addie heard a low "Oh, my God" slip from his lips. Apparently the fear provided enough adrenaline in both Jim and Jean Claude to be able to pull Ian a few feet out of the water. Jim threw several more lines over Ian and fastened them quickly to the cleats, securing him in a hanging position along the side, but high enough out of the water to make the shark turn back out into the waves.

Behind the cockpit, Addie could hear Kit struggling with Barnacle, who was whining frantically as she hoisted his wet body up and over the transom with tremendous strength. Kit had pulled herself up onto the ladder and screamed as she saw the head of a shark moving fast, coming straight up from the water right under her, mouth open, displaying a long row of razor-sharp teeth. Thankfully, it crashed back into the water without dinner. Had she not been looking down, Kit might be missing a leg now, and the sheer terror of the encounter sent her scrawling up onto deck like a lightning bolt. She jumped up, headed to the front of the boat and added her strength to Jim and Jean Claude's, the three of them pulling together to get Ian's legs through the life lines and wedging him halfway on deck. J.C. then pulled Ian's body, now a dead weight, beyond the vertical stanchion standing in the way and rolled him onto the deck. Jim turned Ian flat onto his back, listened for a heartbeat and checked his pulse, which was very slow. Slapping Ian's jaw, Jim was able to get a small reaction and asked Ian if he had any injuries anywhere. Ian shook his head but weakly held up his bleeding hand. Jim and J.C. helped Ian down into the cabin, pulling the wet clothes from his body and wrapping him in boat blankets.

"He's probably in shock and may have hypothermia," said Jim. "He was in that water for a long time and the force of it must have been a terrible strain."

Kit went below and instinctively decided that heating up some water seemed like the thing to do.

J.C. showed Addie how to start the engines and get them back on course for their old heading. He opened the emergency kit and found stick-on heating pads he could place on Ian's extremities to warm them up. Everyone moved about the cabin quietly, acknowledging their dire position so far away from help and without an experienced captain. They had to reach their destination, and fast, or Ian could be in danger. He looked listless and pale, no longer resembling the vibrant, strong captain they knew.

The storm still pounded waves against the bow and the wind howled. Jean Claude was back at the nav station, pulling off the weather-fax and checking their position on the chartplotter. The weather report indicated the storm would pass through by morning, so they only had to manage through the night and get to St. Pierre. Medical facilities were far and few between in the islands, but J.C. felt Ian would be okay if they could make good time. Since Ian was incapacitated, J.C. assumed the role of captain without asking and began to help them regain order regarding their duties. Kit would continue as first mate, Jim would stay on navigation and Addie would shift to galley duties.

Since he knew much more than any of them, this made sense to Addie. She gladly volunteered to take charge of the meals to free Jean Claude up to lead. She rummaged around the galley and found a bag of dried navy beans in the storage locker that would make a good pot of soup. The task of preparing the meal was comforting to her after the terror of the day. She chopped whatever fresh vegetables she could find and added some onion and island spices to the mix. This would be a comforting dinner for a cold and exhausted crew if complete with a bread of some kind, so she dug around in the storage locker and found an unopened box of yellow cornmeal, quickly making up some batter to throw into a cast iron pan that barely fit into the small oven. Before long, the smells alone would comfort the tired crew. The task of hospitality was what she did best. The bean soup with a splash of vinegar would be just the right thing to warm their bodies. Addie planned to serve the cornbread piping hot with a crusty outside layer and fresh butter. She was in her sweet spot doing things for other people, and taking on the role comforted her jittery nerves. *Better than deck swab, any day. We'll have time for that later in port.*

After dinner, all fell into their roles in silence. Jim took the helm. Kit bundled up on the bunk across the parlor to keep an eye on Ian. Jean Claude and Addie retired to their cabins for a much-needed nap before their evening watch. They'd all have to do three-hour watches alone now. Jim was on deck from 6 to 9 p.m., Addie was on again at 9 p.m., then Jean Claude at midnight and Kit the 3 a.m. shift.

Addie's head hurt and her stomach had a dull ache from the constant motion of the boat, but she was too tired to be afraid, so she no longer felt the need to be sick. At least that was progress.

Chapter 16

Addie loved storms. She remembered sitting on the front porch of her grandmother's house and watching the fury of a storm pass through the neighborhood. The thunder and lightning had never seemed frightening in the safety of a warm house or even bundled up in a blanket on the front porch. Being in the middle of this one, with the elements right there in her face, made her feel as alive as it did in her childhood. Seeing Kit's full embrace of the experience at the helm and her brave rescue of Barnacle had left an impression on Addie she'd never forget. Kit was a hero to act in such a bold manner. For that matter, so were Jean Claude and Jim. But Addie? She was always thinking of what's next, of solving problems and troubleshooting harm, instead of living her life the way others did. She envied people who lived so fully in the moment. Kit's physical connection with an immediate situation was seductive, and Addie wanted more of that for herself. The longer she was here, the more she saw how disconnected she'd been from life, in so many ways. No wonder her cat didn't particularly like her. And her plants all eventually died. Now, on-board the *True Tilt*, she was noticing everything in full detail because she couldn't ignore it. *I'm living fully in the moment like I've never done before.* The encounter with the shark had been terrifying, but it somehow made her aware of a bigger world, where people are not the center of it and cannot control it. A world she wanted to know more about.

Twelve hours had passed since the accident, and she'd begun to change in noticeable ways. Her legs felt sturdier and more nimble, her arms had grown stronger, and she was enjoying the luxury of freshly-washed hair dried in the salty wind, giving it texture and a touch of wildness that felt freeing. When she looked at herself in the mirror, she was amazed at the woman looking back. Bright green eyes that looked more confident with each day. Skin brushed with the caramel touch of wind and sun. This woman was vibrant in some fundamental way that matched the spectacular scenery of the surroundings. This was a new Addie and she was beginning to see her own potential in new ways.

She loved everything about the boat, too. Learning the nautical terms, the maneuvers, and duties. Coiling the lines into a perfect circle on the decks with precision, tying the lines so they hung just right on the stanchions. It was all so neat and precise. At some point over the last few days, her inquisitive mind had engaged with learning the art of the sport. She had a million questions and had looked them up in the materials on-board. Aware that Jean Claude was not 100% comfortable being captain, she decided it was important to assume more responsibility herself, so she started assisting him with the many chores aboard the sloop. She was thinking ahead to what might need to be done. She played with the controls at the chartplotter and read the manual when she couldn't figure out the answer to a question. It was like one big grand puzzle!

Jean Claude sensed Addie's newfound interest. He'd begun to delegate tasks that taught her how to involve herself in the routines of life at sea. Her nausea had subsided sometime in the afternoon of the second day, so she'd regained her strength and a newfound composure had set in. Her body was beginning to look and feel different, too. Certain muscle groups had started to relax and let go of control. She was noticing the weather with acute awareness and thinking about how to interact with it, using the parts of the boat to embrace its power to take them to their destination. Always the destination. Always interested in the list of things to get them there.

Over the last 24 hours the five had stopped feeling like strangers. Their behaviors had shifted to something very much like family members who cared about one another. They crowded around the parlor table in the protected cabin for meals, while the raging winds continued circling above deck. Somewhere between days two and three, they'd become a team. Five people with a common destination.

The crew was in better spirits. Ian had a little more color in his face and was looking like he might live. Barnacle had not left his side since the incident. His big brown adoring eyes were fixed on his master and even Addie couldn't tempt him away with a morsel of smoked ham. He seemed aware that the warmth of his body was needed to help his master. Addie decided she needed a dog. Her cat didn't love her like that.

Ian spoke for the first time since his rescue. "I was impressed with how you all came together as a team. I hope you know how much I appreciate your saving me from a treacherous situation. Never had anything like that happen to me before and I have to say, I was close to giving up. The force of the water was pulling me down so hard that staying above for air was the most difficult thing I've ever had to do. Sure am glad you blokes figured out how to fall off. I don't think I would have survived if you hadn't figured that out as quickly as you did."

"Yeah, I was surprised we all came together the way we did too," Jim said. "Kit, you blew me away, saving Barnacle like that, you crazy girl. Jumped right in there with a shark in the water to save an animal."

"Well, I can't say I was consciously thinking about the shark until I was back on the transom, but I did know that damn dog was going to make things worse. AND that I had to get him away from Ian or he was going to be in a heap of trouble. I was afraid Barnacle would push Ian even farther under. I was a lifeguard in college and know a few things about swimming and rescue techniques. So I thought, who the hell else is going to do it?"

"I know what you mean," Jim responded, "cuz I was darned glad today for the first-aid training I had as captain of the basketball team."

Addie wished she was more talented in practical things. She guessed she wasn't much of a hero type. *I need to choose to be braver from now on.*

Just then, Kit said "Well, we can all be grateful to Addie for doing her homework. I didn't know what the hell 'falling off' was. If she hadn't told me, I wouldn't have known what to do and things would have gotten worse quickly! I was cursing myself for not being more diligent about studying the sailing terms handouts!" She looked at Addie with great appreciation. Jean Claude looked intently at Addie too. She wondered what he was thinking.

"When crews go through storms together and survive, it creates a bond that can never be broken," said Ian. "There's a hero in all of us and when people save one another, they're connected for life. Bet you guys didn't know that, eh? Bloody big responsibility, saving a bloke's life! Now you're stuck with me!" It was good to see Ian smiling again.

Chapter 17

Seth could not believe his luck. The stockholders meeting had gone much easier than he'd anticipated. He had a silver tongue, a pedigree education and everything he touched seemed to work in his favor. This included the stroke of luck a few weeks ago, when the old guy dropped dead, with no warning whatsoever. Dellwood had been the only obstacle left. Seth's goal was to become CEO by the age of 40. He would soon achieve that, and before his 39th birthday. He'd been thinking about how he could get rid of the old guy, a pawn in his plan, and now that was taken care of by nature itself.

He congratulated himself on a well-executed plan. With years of hard work, combined with his brilliant financial mind, he'd pulled off the plan to buy three major hotel chains. As CFO, he'd masterminded the structure of the deal and negotiated all the relationships that had to be manipulated to pull off such a transaction. And it wasn't over yet. He still had one chain to buy, which would complete the final step in the plan. To keep the scheme working in such a dismal economic environment, he'd need the influx of cash from South America. He knew where the money came from and what it funded, but he didn't have to think about that. The chain of hotels in the Caribbean would be the ideal way to funnel the money without raising suspicion among the more sophisticated companies that would soon be under his control.

He'd decided it was best to keep himself above all the details that might be troublesome. The money would end up going to good use and that was all that mattered. Nicolai had the dirty work all under control, so Seth could focus on his end of the bargain. They'd agreed Nicolai would disappear after the final transaction was complete. Some of the funds would buy him a hotel in Trinidad.

Coming up with a substantial sum of cash had been necessary to convince Dellwood to sign over controlling interest in the private equity firm because he was dying. It had taken his best persuasion skills to prove he could put some skin in the game himself and the old man had acquiesced in his final days, much to the angst of the board and Dellwood's family.

Seth was focused in the mirror, practicing the speech he'd give on his tour around the world, after the final business was transacted in a few weeks. The luxurious hotel suite was something he would never take for granted. He'd grown up in Queens, raised by his single mother who was a seamstress. Now, in a different place and time of his own making, a tailor was measuring his inseam for the custom-made suits he was known for. His sharp good looks and tall stature were made for expensive suits and executive command. He'd imagined this as a boy when his mother sent him to school in handmade clothing that brought only ridicule. Only he knew that the irony of his choice for custom-made clothes was one of the small things that kept him close to her.

He'd secured his speechwriter's expensive services for the entire world tour, and she'd outdone herself with one of the most inspiring keynotes he'd ever delivered. She said he was her best student, the crowning joy of her own career. As the tailor finished, he practiced the altruistic words in his mind, over and over, giving them just the right emotional inflections. Make them laugh and then make them cry, that's what he loved most. He had to win the enthusiastic support of thousands of employees, ensuring him total emotional control. He'd made it to his goal of achieving status and power, but that wouldn't be enough unless he could also have their complete admiration. It was the applauding crowds he needed the most. And soon it would all be his.

Chapter 18

Jean Claude squinted, looking into the binoculars. "Martinique should be in view by now. With the heading we've been on, we should have seen land much earlier. I checked our position and something's off." Ian picked up the concern in J.C.'s voice and rummaged around under the nav desk, pulling out paper charts of the Windward Islands.

The bad weather had continued, with poor visibility. They'd been sailing for twenty-four hours since the accident and were well beyond their estimated destination time. The currents and wind had carried them off course during the accident, but they'd corrected the headings.

"Could be we've somehow missed the island," said Ian, making calculations by hand and checking them against the autopilot and chartplotter. "Something's definitely wrong. We should be within a mile of St. Pierre and I don't see signs of land anywhere. Let's come about and see if we can find her. Gotta be that we missed her. She's a big island, but it's hard to see beyond our nose right now."

"Okay, coming about!" Kit announced. The sails were out of the tilt position and angrily slapped about to find the wind on the other reach. Once positioned, she went right back into the tilt of the wind and headed toward the island's charted longitude and latitude.

Hours passed and still no island. Tacking back and forth, it became clear the GPS was not registering correct readings. Ian suddenly remembered he'd experienced this once before, and knew what the problem might be. A metallic object! He began searching the cabin, pulling everything apart and out – cushions, cabinets, clothing. Nothing!

"What's he doing?" Jim half thought Ian had lost it.

"I'm looking for a metal object that may have become magnetized. It sometimes happens. Metal that has become magnetic can pull the autopilot off a few degrees and mess up the readings. That's the only explanation left, unless Martinique has become the next Atlantis!"

"The key! I'll bet it's the key! " yelled Kit. She finally admitted to the secret she'd been keeping to herself. "Look under the cushion in my cabin, Ian. There's a great big key that looks like it goes to a castle. A woman gave it to me on the way here."

A few minutes later, Ian came into the cockpit with a Cheshire Cat grin. "You bet that's it!" He held an ancient key that had to be six inches long and looked like it weighed three pounds.

"Holy Smoke," Addie said. "That is some key you've got there, Kit."

"When were you going to tell us about this?" Jim asked in a teasing voice.

"Well, I didn't know what it was for, and I planned to tell you. Of course I did!" Kit defended herself with a little mischief in her smile.

Raring back his arm to throw the key into the ocean, Ian looked over to Kit as if to ask permission.

"NOOOO!" Kit shrieked. "Don't you dare throw that in the ocean! We don't know how important it may be!"

Jim agreed and Addie chimed in, too. They had a couple of items that might go with that key, so none of the group was willing to toss what might be important to their secret adventure.

"Okay," said Ian, "but we're going to have to wrap it up and move it, so it doesn't interfere with the nav equipment again. I'm taking it into custody until we get to our final destination."

"Awe, you don't need to do that," whined Kit. But she quickly conceded, though carefully watching Ian as he went below and into the aft cabin.

Two hours later, the storm subsided and the sun poked out, warming up the sky just as the day was ending. With the autopilot working, they'd headed in the right direction long enough to sight Martinique's silhouette. Ian gave instructions about dropping anchor in the bay at St. Pierre. They'd arrive within the hour but because they were approaching at such a late hour, would grab a mooring ball in the bay for the night. The waves had grown smaller and the sight of land lifted their spirits substantially. They'd refuel in the morning. Excitement was in the air.

Chapter 19

As they pulled into the large mouth of the bay at sunset, the juxtaposition of St. Mary's statue and a towering volcano on the left struck Addie as polar opposites. The yin and yang of life, the Nurturer and the Destroyer each holding vigil over the passersby, into and out of the port of St. Pierre, Martinique.

Reading the navigation guidebook, Addie learned that the Windward Isles of the West Indies were a potluck of islands, each settled by different explorers. This one was owned by the French, its mother country's influence evident as they pulled into the aqua blue lagoon close to shore. Even from a distance, a rich Catholic presence created the notion that a religious order had been brought here to tame this barbaric land across the sea. The Nurturer had won the battle and the island was at peace, with Saint Mary overlooking her domain.

The crew straightened up the cabin below and showered for dinner. They'd soon be on land again and their rising energy created a palpable exuberance.

"We only have one day in port, so we all have chores to accomplish while we're here," said Ian in his old commanding voice.

"Awe, no way!" Kit exclaimed. "We need a break, *Capitan*! It's time for some rum drinks or French wine and fine French cuisine. Maybe even a little dancing while we're at it!" She winked at Addie as if they had a secret between them.

Jim chimed in. "Yeah, we're due a nice night out, Ian. We had a rough trip and I'm ready for a big steak, *au jus*, of course, and some *frites*!"

To their delight Jean Claude added in his deep baritone, "Ian, ole chap, even you need a little fun every now and then. You had a rough time of it, my friend, and we all deserve an evening of island pleasure. I insist!"

"Well, good enough, then," agreed Ian. "A night out for dinner. But that means our chores will have to be accomplished in the next hour with a short excursion to shore for provisions tonight before dinner and again in the morning when the local market opens. Crack of dawn it will be, so no hangovers, mind you!"

"Yoo, hoo!" Jim hooped and clapped J.C. on the shoulder. "Let's go. The sun's dropping fast! What do we need to knock out before heading to shore?"

When the crew finished the duties Ian had barked out, Ian and Jean Claude lowered the tender into the water and mounted the outboard motor onto the back. The small craft called *Near Tilt* sported the same color scheme as the *True Tilt* mother ship, but was many times smaller. Addie wondered, as she looked at the little skipper, how all five of the adults were going to fit into the tiny thing. The *True Tilt* was attached to a mooring ball in the center of the bay, so apparently this was the "car" that would get them to shore. The bay was speckled with at least a dozen other boats but the dark blue Hinckley dwarfed the others and was, without question, the superior yacht of the group.

Once settled into the *Near Tilt*, they were preparing to head to land when Ian whistled loudly. Barnacle leapt off of the rear deck, landing smack in the middle of the tender.

Kit moaned, "Oh, noooo, he's going? How are we going to have a nice dinner with him along, Ian?"

Jean Claude saved Ian from having to defend his best friend. "Come on, gang, he's just as anxious as we are for a real appointment with land and grass. This ole boy's been doing his duty on the fake grass patch for days and loves it when we hit land. Really something to see."

"Indeed, and don't worry about dinner," said Ian. "I have business to attend to with my friend, Gabrielle, and he can stay with her until we're ready to come back to the boat. Gabby is expecting me shortly."

The sun was setting and the peaceful blue water lapped at the edges of the *Near Tilt*. Addie's heart pounded with exhilaration. Happy to be near land again, she felt free to fully enjoy being so intimate with nature and with the small group of people. She had never felt so alive.

As they pulled the tender up to the long, storm-battered dock, Jim tied the painter lines to a piling. Ian and J.C. gave them directions to several small houses on the cliff side. They'd arrived too late for that day's market, but could buy some staples straight from the vendors at their homes tonight, saving time in the morning to market for fresh foods. They were to take tonight's provisions back to the yacht before returning to meet the others for dinner at 9 p.m. Ian instructed them on what to say, so they wouldn't get an argument. Apparently he was well known in these parts and had some influence. Specifically, he wanted some baguettes made by Mama Lafitte and wanted the order placed tonight for pickup at the market the next day. Addie noticed that shopping in the islands was an orchestration and not the simple process she was used to back home.

Climbing up the steep incline, they all broke out in sweat from the still-humid heat left over from the hot Caribbean sun. As they approached the porch of the small cottage where Mama lived, the smell of freshly baked bread and the sweet aroma of banana nut emanated from the kitchen. The woman frowned and wiped sweat from her brow as she opened the door. Her apron was covered in dust from the flour.

Jim and Kit were negotiating their provisions with Mama Lafitte when Addie was drawn to look at the bay. It was now almost dark, but in the distance, she could still make out their yacht where it was moored. Though she might be imagining things, she felt certain the big white boat with the black windows was pulled up close behind the *True Tilt*. Squinting her eyes, she tried to focus. Heart pounding, she shouted to Jim and Kit to come take a look. But by the time they collected their change from Mama, it had grown too dark to see anything. Jim reassured her it was probably a trick of the eye from that distance. Addie decided it was her overactive sense of caution again and chided herself for being a worrier.

The three walked in the warm, balmy night back down the hill to the dock. Jim volunteered to run the provisions back to the *True Tilt* and left the two women to wait for him. It was eerily quiet except for several teenage boys lounging along the dock, talking softly among themselves. In any other place, Addie would have felt nervous. She thought the cigarettes the boys were smoking smelled suspiciously like something else. But she was becoming used to the two opposite aspects of island life there, the quiet beauty and the wild passion juxtaposed. Life held more extremes here.

On the edge of town, Kit noticed a stand with t-shirts, tube tops and sarongs. Pulling Addie by the arm, she dragged her over to shop for a few minutes while they waited for Jim. Kit's idea was to find a couple of tube tops and sarongs that complimented one another for the gals to wear that night to dinner.

"Wouldn't it be delectable to have something feminine to wear tonight, Addie? I am sick to death of these shorts and polos we have to wear every day. Are you in?"

"Well, I do like this one that has an animal print and it would look good with a black top." She was tempted, thinking about Jean Claude.

"Well, let's do it! I have some cash in my pocket and I am sure we can bargain for a good price." Kit picked out a sarong with swirling shades of green and a dark green top. Against her dark red hair, the colors looked wonderful on her, thought Addie. She tucked the package under her arm, intending to change in the ladies room at the restaurant. *Why not? Just one more out-of-character experience I can indulge in just for fun.*

When Jim returned and tied up the boat, Addie noticed he looked a little distracted. His brow was knit in deep thought as he asked the local boys for directions to the French restaurant Ian had said was up the long set of stone stairs. She would have to ask Jim about it later.

The city was bright with lights and the excitement of impending nightlife gave energy to the air. They climbed the long sets of stairs and eventually found *La Petite Paris*. Ian and Jean Claude were seated at a large table in the corner of the open-air restaurant and apparently deep in conversation. Addie and Kit headed to the ladies room to change and returned in a flash. Jim immediately noticed the change of attire as he escorted the ladies to the table, and acknowledged it with a simple raised eyebrow and appreciative smile.

The three joined Ian and Jean Claude who had already ordered two bottles of French wine for the table. Jean Claude took on the role of host and poured wine into their glasses, explaining the qualities of the wines he had chosen. They raised their glasses to a toast and a memorable evening between friends began.

"This place is so strange, Ian," Jim said. "Why do they have so many ancient-looking stairs and ruins like Greece?"

"Very astute of you, ole chap. There is indeed a captivating story in the history of this place. Sit down and I'll tell you the story."

He told them St. Pierre had been discovered by Christopher Columbus in 1502 but had not been settled until the mid 1600's. Fast becoming the "Little Paris of the West Indies," it was the most promising and popular of the islands in the 17th century. With a growing population from all over the world, its European and Asian settlers came to reap the benefits of the sugarcane industry. After the 1848 abolishment of slavery, the European descendents called the Beké switched their efforts to a more cost-effective use of their thriving sugarcane industry, becoming the first Caribbean Rum exporter in the world. The African population grew and eventually became predominant, so the Beké and a small contingent of French Europeans were only a 5% minority of the current population.

"Is the island an independent country?" asked Kit.

"No, its still part of France and in the European Union. That's why the currency here is the Euro."

"Why all the ruins?" Jim was still not satisfied he had an answer to that mystery.

"Oh, that! Yes, the most important part of the history of St. Pierre. Did you notice the volcano? Well, this used to be *little Paris*. Before the 1902 eruption of Mount Pelé, that is. She blew up and wiped out the entire town, a population of more than 28,000 with only one survivor, a prisoner who stayed alive under the jailhouse. The town had been wiped out once before when the Great Hurricane of 1780 destroyed the city and its 8000 inhabitants. Some thought they'd been cursed for distributing the devil's rum. Thank goodness those old superstitions didn't last." Ian toasted to the good rum he was drinking.

"Here, here," joined Jim. Everyone clinked glasses and broke into individual conversations about St. Pierre's history. Addie was fascinated, and asked Ian to say more about the statues and ruins.

There had been a theatre and all of the accoutrements of high-class life in the late 1800's. "How tragic that it's all in ruins now," Ian said. "The activity of volcanoes was not well-known in those days, so the governor had assured everyone the city was safe because of the ravines at the base of the mountain. He'd convinced them all to cluster with him in the city center and they'd all died instantly from the extreme gushes of fumes and heat. The lava was last, finishing off the city structures."

"So, Ian, how do you know so much about this place?" inquired Kit.

"Well, I come here often to see Gabby. We're good friends and I'll be off to have dinner with Gabby and Barnacle, so I'll leave you in the good hands of Jean Claude. But before I leave, I have a surprise for you. We have a guest arriving for this last leg of the trip. Jean Claude will introduce you to him and explain who he is. He's going to catch a ride back to Mayreau with us tomorrow and it should be quite the treat. He's well known in these parts, and world-renowned with sailors. He's dropped out of the race and now lives a quiet life in Mayreau." With that, he turned his eyes to Jean Claude, and bid them all good night.

Chapter 20

Dinner was over and the staccato beating of the steel drum was calling people to the dance. Several locals were moving their bodies to the beat of the primal sound of the music, dancing alone and oblivious to the onlookers. One blonde Beké woman, draped in a white sarong, writhed her hips, eyes closed and clearly oblivious to anyone who might be watching.

Kit could not contain her own instinctual response. She was up and dancing next to the blonde, letting her body play with the percussion sounds until she was in sync with the island music. Addie again wished she were more like Kit. In that moment of hesitation, Jean Claude suddenly pulled her to the floor and guided her close, so he could teach her the rhythm of the music. Not wanting to be left out, Jim joined Kit on the floor and they all fell into the intoxication of island *ojo*, where so many pleasures converge – good food, friendship, wine and music. The four lost themselves in the damp, sultry air of the Caribbean evening.

An hour passed before the musicians stopped and they came back to their table, drenched and exhilarated. Nearby, a table of French Legionnaires clanked their mugs together and belted out a soldier's song in unison. They'd been holding a contest and were rowdy and competitive. The winner had held a full glass of wine in the upright position on his forehead for more than fifteen minutes without dropping it. As the glass finally began to fall, the next challenger grabbed it in midair.

In the midst of this, Jean Claude ordered a new bottle of good French wine, poured four glasses and proposed another toast to his new friends, then began to explain, "We are here for a very special reason, and I need to tell you about it tonight. Here's to our success!" Normally quiet, almost brooding and always composed, tonight Jean Claude exuded certainty and purpose. "We are here to help someone very important to me. His name is Nate. The four of us were chosen as the team of people who can best help the local government and the NGO coordinate a creative solution to the problems they've faced for the past decade. A crisis has arisen as a result of recent happenings, and time is of great concern now. We're each uniquely qualified to help Nate and Ian lead this effort to a sustainable solution. We had to use our connections to get you all here, and I can only hope you will sense the privilege it is to be a part of this."

"Who is this Nate fellow, J.C.?" Kit was the curious consultant already, wanting to know the status of those she supported.

"Nathaniel Drake. To put it simply, he's very special to me, mostly because he saved my life," said J.C. "You might remember my telling you that when I lost Jane, I signed up for the Whitbread around-the-world race. Nate was our captain. That was the year I began to look at the world in a whole new way. Largely because of Nate's leadership and years of wisdom, I was able to put myself back together. I owe him my life and would give it for him if he asked. He has requested our help and I hope you will listen carefully, for the sake of solving their dilemma, but even more importantly for yourselves. His wisdom is something you won't want to miss. He has a way of knowing exactly what you need to learn. He's one of those people who speak wisdom with so little effort; you know it's part of him."

"I'm intrigued," said Jim. "A little wisdom, I could use right now. Any help I can get I will certainly borrow." He was thinking about what he faced back home. He'd made a mess of things by being duplicitous. It was sinking in.

"Me too," echoed Kit. "Sebastian sent me here for a reason and I'm listening." She'd been thinking for days of what Sebastian said when she left – that she needed to listen more, develop some sensitivity; that her overly certain arrogance was evidence she 'didn't know what she didn't know'. Her colleagues had complained to him that she seemed to have a problem with entitlement and put forward the ideas and work of others as her own, taking credit and not honoring the hard work and sacred creativity of others. People thought she was overly ambitious, dismissive and aggressive. She didn't realize she did this at all and denied it, so he gave her numerous examples. It had been a real pill to swallow. Her mind was still racing with rationalizations for her actions. Accepting the feedback felt intolerable. She had to guard against it. Just thinking about it sent her into an internal rage against those who had complained about her. *But Sebastian sent me here for a reason...*

Jean Claude interrupted her thoughts, "Very few people have access to Nate anymore, so you're quite fortunate to have this kind of time with him. There's an old saying that when someone becomes a sage, that person either becomes world-renowned, or walks off into the sunset to live a quiet life. This particular man has done both. He's a world-renowned sailor who's won the Whitbread more times by far than anyone else." He paused for a moment and added; "Though Addie and Kit will enjoy the fact that his record may be surpassed by Clare one day soon, if she wins another two. She was a rigger and his first mate on our yacht four years ago. Nate's a master at building teams and inspiring new leaders to take on challenges of their own. I think he's one of the greatest leaders you'll ever know personally. He became so sought after by admirers that he just disappeared one day. No one has heard from him in four years, so it must be a matter of importance if he's reached out to us for help." J.C. finished speaking and let this information sink in.

"Well, spit it out, mate!" Jim said, mimicking Ian's favorite endearment. "We've been waiting for this for a week now!"

Responding to the urgency she often experienced when feeling vulnerable, Kit threw one leg over the other and her top foot started tapping furiously against the table leg. She used to refer to this urgency as "The Great Clock," often joking that it ticked inside her chest instead of a heart. That had been a good thing when the "tough consultant" was needed to give the tough messages to clients, but lately Sebastian had chided her for such comments. Out of impulse she suddenly said, "I hope we can get to the bottom of this quickly, because I have one of the biggest assignments of my career waiting back home and I'm not supposed to go back until this little excursion is over." Just as she'd said it, she knew she sounded trite and impatient. *Why did that pop out of my mouth without my permission?* She felt a little embarrassed. It was a strange new feeling to second guess yourself when you've never done so before.

Kit's comments made Addie a little uncomfortable. Didn't she sense this was important to Jean Claude? She was always thinking of her own perspective and didn't seem very in tune with others for some odd reason. "Go on, Jean Claude," Addie said.

"Well, there is a little history you will need first. So, sit back and listen while you drink this last bottle with me. Nate will be here before long and I want you to have the background before he arrives."

~~~

Across the room from them, Nicolai sat in a dark corner watching the happy group with disgust. He'd tried to board the *True Tilt* earlier and it had been locked. He would have to find a way to get that map from Jean Claude. It was his destiny and his time. No one was going to stand in his way.

Chapter 21

Addie scanned hundreds of emails on her iPhone while she waited for everyone to get ready to go ashore. Several appeared important and she'd been looking for an opportunity to make a call back to the mainland. Her boss had written to share news of the chaos back at the corporate offices. The private equity conglomerate's purchase of their brands was apparently interrupted by the sudden death of the company's owner. The papers had not been signed and dozens of lawyers were working to ascertain the acquisition's status.

He wanted Addie to come back from her trip as soon as she got the message that his job had been eliminated along with the other three Executive Vice Presidents of Ops, and the COO was calling a special strategy meeting. She'd been invited to come and David was asked to let her know. She had a few moments to break away from dinner, and stepped outside to make the call away from the primal pounding of the steel drums. "David, I got your message."

"Geez, Addie, where the hell are you?" She could barely hear him.

"Oh, in a restaurant. Let me walk down the street away from the noise. What's up? I got your message that things are going haywire back there?" Addie felt a pang of guilt for not being at work.

"Yeah, all hell's broken loose. I don't have time to tell you much, but if you don't want to be left out of the politics going on here, you'd better jump on the first plane to Memphis. You need to be part of the discussions if you want to protect your interests. I don't have time to explain, but I've been offered a move to the gaming division, and the other VPs have been let go. The COO is determined to restructure and if you're not here, no one will be sticking up for you. I'm just saying Addie, if I were you, I'd get back here."

"But David, why am I even here right now? Are you sure I'm supposed to come back?" Addie was confused because she thought the company had sent her here. Obviously, the wind had changed since she left the conference.

He interrupted her. "All I can tell you is things are unstable here. You need to be able to make your move now and…."

"Thanks for calling David. I'll let you know." Addie showed no doubt in her voice. There was some important reason she was here and she wasn't ready to make that decision just yet.

"Look Addie, I'm saying this could cost you big money if you don't bust your hump and get back here to protect your territory. They're like sharks around here, and the word is that the COO might have a place for you on the team but wants to know where the hell you are. It's what you've always wanted and since they're moving me over to another business unit, I suggested you for EVP of the Southeastern Region." His voice had changed. When he was taking credit for something that wasn't true, his voice sounded too self-promoting. Addie considered his words. *What is he up to?*

"Thanks David, I don't know what I'm going to do. I'm in no position to hop a plane at the moment, so it's going to have to wait until I get back to the main island airport. I'll be in touch." The phone went dead and she let the signal disconnect them before they'd said a proper goodbye. With a certainty she rarely felt, she knew she could not go back right now. This was a defining moment, her first chance to take a different road. She'd always been the responsible one who put work first. Strangely, she was being offered exactly what she'd sought for years, and she felt indifferent. *Maybe this was what Ian called a tempter? Someone who wants you to do what you are good at, but it takes you away from what you really want to do that requires a personal risk?*

Addie called Emma's cell. She wanted to hear her daughter's voice and learn how "summer camp" at Emma's grandparents was going. It felt good just to do something different. Something felt right about it. Scary as hell, but right.

Chapter 22

Marissa lit a kerosene lamp and carefully placed it in the windowsill in her room on Jamosa Street in Old Wall Village. Waiting by the window, she could hear the echo of children playing a block away. Her feet had walked the steep, winding street so often she could make her way from end to end with her eyes closed. She knew everyone on this small island of little more than 300 inhabitants. Unlike the others, however, she longed to see beyond it. Her mother and most of her family had never been off of the island, but Marissa planned to see the world. At sixteen, she felt she'd waited for decades, though it had only been since she was eleven.

She worked at the Saltwhistle Bay Resort store where they sold t-shirts, trinkets, ice and fresh baked bread to the yachties in Saltwhistle Bay. Each morning on her way to work she walked to the top of the hill above town. If she was early enough, she would stop for fifteen minutes of quiet in the old Church on the hill. In the wooden pew of the small stone church, she made her wishes known to the Mother Mary, bowed on her knees for a few minutes of confession, then walked quickly to the resort on the other side of the hill to work long days alongside her other family members who worked there, too. Always with an eye on the bay, she waited for the boat she longed to see on the horizon. On breaks she would sit on the beach and look for his boat in the bay. She had been waiting for him to come home for so long now and she still held hope. Her faith came from weekly letters left in the offering plate on Sundays to appeal to a God she believed watched over them. Sometimes the requests were for others, sometimes for her wishes, but *always for him*. He was her love and her life.

At the resolve of another long day that was always the same, Marissa lit the lamp again as the sun descended into blackness. She opened the familiar old book with the cracked leather cover and read the sacred words that gave her hope. Hope that one day, he would come back home. Her small, sun-darkened fingers turned the pages carefully. The words calmed her and comforted her restless heart once again. He would come. She was sure of it. She left the lamp burning until it was the last light on the island. As always, somewhere around 3 a.m. her eyelids would droop with exhaustion and, finally, sleep would come.

PART FOUR

THE SAGE

Wisdom ~ **The call of truth widens perspective, and the Ruler becomes the Sage.**

"Great wisdom is the judgment that comes from years of wrestling with great questions."

- Pam Boney

Chapter 23

Several hours later the sun rose over the blue bay, waking the slumbering crew to the morning duties of provisioning. Ian sounded a whistle and barked out instructions to his slightly hung-over patrons. Orders had been doled out the night before and the crew had to get ice and fresh produce provisions at the town market. Ian and Jean Claude would meet Nate at the dock to take on fuel and water for the last leg of the trip to Mayreau. The crew boarded the *Near Tilt*, for the trip to shore and were met with a scene very different from the evening before. The town bustled with activity as the market vendors organized their goods. Ladies of the night became sellers of produce by day and the crew bargained for the provisions on their list. Ian had tasked them with making good use of the boat money, saying they'd need to make thrifty deals to complete the list efficiently. Ripe fruit, fresh fish, a wide range of vegetables and French cheeses covered the market tables under the tent. Once they'd completed their purchases, they headed back to the dock to prepare for the final leg of their voyage. Ian had moved the *True Tilt* alongside the fuel dock and boat boys were lining up to offer last minute services for a fee.

As they approached the dock, Addie once again noticed the rather stunning and intimidating stature of the man called Nate. His regal head was full of white hair, his tanned skin striking, and his steel-blue eyes so intense she felt he could see straight into her soul. Although he was considerably older than everyone, he did not appear to have lost any of his vitality or power. When he'd joined them for a final drink the night before at La Petite Paris, she'd been impressed with the raw power of his presence and so, it seemed, had the others. He exuded confidence and wisdom like no one she'd ever met. Even Kit had been quiet, taken with his ability to focus the conversation on the important task he cared so much about. The encounter had been short, but added noticeable excitement and anticipation to the adventure in front of them. He'd expressed his genuine appreciation to each of them for coming to help with the dilemma, and most especially to Ian and Jean Claude for pulling them together. The voyage had shifted to a more serious tone that stirred Addie deeply. And, unlike other situations that seemed important in the night but changed in the light of day, the feeling still lingered this morning.

The locals on the dock bustled around the *True Tilt*, preparing her for departure. Tanks full of fuel and water, provisions loaded into the galley and stowed in lockers, they were almost ready to go. When Ian whistled loudly, Barnacle jumped onto the dock from the beach and waited to be hosed down before boarding. Sitting alert by his master's side, he allowed himself to be soaked to rid his bristly hair of sand. With a full-body shake, Barnacle jumped on-board and bounded to the bow to find his spot on the bowsprit.

"Boy has his habits," Ian chuckled. "All on-board and off we go."

"Yes, let's get on with it," agreed Kit, always ready to go.

Addie felt something in the air had changed. With Nate on-board, Ian and Jean Claude seemed different – full of energy but also at full attention and in command of that energy. Even Jim and Kit seemed more fully engaged with the voyage. Jean Claude's story last night had given the trip a whole new meaning.

Ian revved the engine and steered her out of port, the winds whipping up as they rounded the corner of the bay. To capture the fifteen knots they unfurled the sails, which made a loud FLOP as they opened. Jim was at the nav, plotting the course to Mayreau. Jean Claude let out the genoa sail and Barnacle hunkered down on the bowsprit, nose to the wind. Kit and Addie removed the fenders and placed them in the deck lockers, fastened the lifelines, then wound and knotted the dock lines the way Ian had taught them.

They were underway and the weather was fair. Addie could not remember a day when she felt more in tune with nature. The great vessel responded to the sea and the wind, rocking in a motion that caressed her soul. The whooshing of the waves against the freeboard reminded her of the peaceful sound of waves washing ashore on the beach. All her senses came to life and her body finally relaxed into the motion. Even her jaw, normally tight, loosened noticeably. Her stomach had settled, too. She deftly moved about the precarious deck and cabin with easy steps now. She was beginning to know herself in a new way. And she liked the change.

Ian said they would have a perfect sail for the journey, with fifteen knots of wind on a broad reach by day, then clocking around for a downwind sail later in the evening. Ian explained that this day was the perfect experience of "True Tilt," meaning the vessel was in her sweet spot, making best use of the weather conditions and tilting into the wind for maximum efficacy to get to the true destination.

~~~

At the end of a glorious day of fair-weather sailing, the sun was beginning to set and the cool breeze drew everyone on deck for the most compelling part of any day at sea. Jean Claude had whipped up a delicious Mahi dish with curry sauce, mushrooms and rice for dinner from a recipe he'd borrowed from friends in Antigua.

"We truly had a jolly good day for a sail," offered Ian.

"Indeed we did, Ian, and thank you for ordering a good breeze for the leg where I could join you," said Nate. He smiled broadly, lines spreading widely at the corners of his eyes.

"We're due for a good, easy downwind sail this voyage," said Ian. "We're full sail and True Tilt into the wind, with easy seas at 3-4 feet for two days at least, and hopefully we'll arrive before it changes. The radar looks clear for miles around us and the weather-fax indicates no instability anywhere near. This will give us plenty of time to fill in the blanks and have a good chat about the task at hand for our meeting on Mayreau."

"At last, a downwind heading to ease all our woes," said Jean Claude, "and especially mine, because I haven't been back to Mayreau since I lost Jane." It troubled him to revisit emotions he'd successfully suppressed for years. To the others he said, "I fear the jog to my memory will be more than I can bear, but Nate says I must go back and complete the purpose of our being there."

Ian, the instigator of healing for his good friend, added encouragement. "Nate's right, J.C. Going back is the only way to wrestle the demons that plague you. There's a purpose to all of it we can't yet understand. Your future is ahead of you, mate. And you have all of us with you this time. Our emotions aren't nearly as treacherous as our minds might fear when we go head-on into them. You're stronger than you realize."

"Well," Jim added, "we're all here for some reason. I can feel it in my bones." Jim thought about his dilemma back home and felt his own core strength beginning to change as he observed his new friends facing challenges of their own. Being in the visceral experience of nature was also helping him think more clearly. He was beginning to believe he, too, could face his own demons head-on.

Chapter 24

Onandi had left Mayreau after his family held the memorial service for his younger brother. He'd taken his late father's oldest fishing boat and left immediately following the ceremony. His eldest brother and two uncles, the best fishermen in the village, would look after his mother and two sisters. At first he'd searched weeks for the tourist responsible for his brother's death. He asked questions until he found what he needed to know, then wandered around listlessly for a month before meeting Brother King on Union Island. Numb from the pain of his loss and tired from weeks of fishing without success, Onandi was hungry and exhausted, begging from tourists on the streets, when Brother offered him work on Bequia.

A retired fisherman himself, Brother had founded a non-profit turtle sanctuary to fight against extinction of sea turtles which only have a 5% chance of survival on their own. The sanctuary partnered with people on many islands in the lower Caribbean, collecting baby turtles as they hatched, nurturing them for two years, then releasing them back into the ocean. Brother's passion for his work and the seeming importance of it had attracted Onandi, who felt nothing but lost and hopeless. The match had been a good one.

On Bequia, Onandi found new purpose. He was charged with placing barriers around turtle egg nests locals had found on the beaches, protecting them until hatching. Tonight he was at watch on one site, where a full moon increased the likelihood the eggs would hatch before dawn. His job was to collect the babies and take them by boat to their new home at Old Hegg. There he would care for them until they were two, as the good Brother King had taught him. He wasn't paid much, especially since the hurricane had affected funding, but he didn't care. Here he did something that mattered. Taking care of them, helping them heal when they were sick, had given him a reason to live in spite of his anger and grief.

Onandi's brown skin glistened with sweat from the long walk to the deserted beach. He sat quietly under the full moon and allowed himself to think about the one thing he'd kept buried in the cavern of his past. *Marissa. If it weren't for her, I would never go back.* The image of her face had grown stronger in his mind, reminding him how much he had left behind. His desire to run away was slowly being replaced by a desire for something stronger.

Chapter 25

Ian had asked Nate to tell some of his sailing lore, and the conversation eventually digressed into a philosophical discussion about life and leadership of vessels.

"So Nate, tell us the secrets of winning races." Jim was intrigued by the records the man had behind him.

"Ah, no secrets mate. Just wisdom about the principles of nature, and how we interact with it, as well as some measure of luck. Alas, we give too much credit to the Captain for the win, as well as too much blame for the loss, when there are so many uncontrollables at play in the race."

"Come on, don't be so humble my friend. Tell them some of your captain's wisdom, Nate." Jean Claude happily anticipated the retelling of his old mentor's stories.

"Well, okay J.C., if you wish. Leadership is truly an important phenomenon in terms of the effect on the team's morale especially, and that morale is one of the most important variables indeed. Probably most important for the captain is knowing first, who you are and second, how you fit into the world. Great captains must know themselves, know what they value, know their personal limitations, have command of their own actions and have an idea of where they're going. They must know their own truth above all else, for if they lose themselves, they've already lost the journey. They must find their own True Tilt. The one that works for *them*, but is also in sync with the principles of nature. Some are more adventurous, some more observant, some more visionary, some more diplomatic and so on. This kind of truth comes only with wisdom. And wisdom gives rise to confidence and powerful presence."

Kit asked, "Yes, but what exactly is 'wisdom,' Nate? Everyone says that, but what does it mean to have it?"

"Well, let me think a moment." Nate paused to consider what he might share with this young group. "Wise leaders must be able to see from many perspectives. They need to expand their own capacity to think from all angles of a situation and also recognize the limitations of any one viewpoint, seeking perspective from others. All novel creators build on the ideas and backs of countless leaders before them. Wisdom is the collection of what we know from history, balanced with what we can imagine about the future. Imagine a ship's crew attempting to navigate the huge challenge of changing seas and weather on the way to a destination. Perspective includes being able to see outside one's own narrow view and being ready for anything. I can keep my focus on a destination, but I must be prepared for surprises."

"For example," Nate continued, "I may have a strong desire to go to Madeira next week, yet Mother Nature may not cooperate with me – perhaps the wind is going in the wrong direction. I can get there but it won't be pretty because the wind is not in my favor. That takes a certain kind of grit and persistence and will. The complexities of the universe are a great puzzle and wise captains engage with those complexities as they arise but also incorporate what they've learned about their environment. For the journey to unfold at its best, you must stay present with and attend to the most important point in time. NOW. Too much focus on the destination can be sure death when at sea. Focusing on the past can be treacherous if dwelling on mistakes erodes confidence to manage current challenges. You keep your eye on the destination, and look for the perfect "true" tilt so you arrive before your competitors. But how you make the journey may be more important in the end. If you cheat nature or one another to get there, it's as if you never arrived at all."

"So, Nate," asked Addie, "you're saying what happens today is more important than the final goal?"

"Not exactly. I'm saying BOTH are important. The essential operating premise in ANY situation is to consider everything on the time continuum — the past informs the present, the present creates the future, and the future is what makes the present so important. Things are not as simple as a secret, or a formula. One must think creatively in every aspect of leadership."

Kit was a strong believer in her own gut instinct for answers. "You speak of thinking. What about emotion and intuition, Nate?"

"Without emotion, we wouldn't need one another and would live independent lives with no meaning. Unless driven and nurtured by emotion, the team has no values and the mission has no purpose. The ship with an emotionally-divided crew will sink. And the crack of division will have been caused by the captain who didn't know the role of emotion in leading a team to its destination. If a captain doesn't manage the extreme aspects of his personality and tilts too far into those extremes, then the crew will sense his or her lack of balance. Another leader will then rise up a faction against the Captain and then the crew becomes divided. The crew is then focused on politics and power instead of the voyage and often the captain is unaware that mutiny is afoot because no one wants to be the messenger. And a divided crew always loses the race. In contrast, when a captain stands as an example to admire, a crew's love and admiration will bring out their best selves and they will follow that captain to the ends of the earth. To respond powerfully to great challenges, leaders must inspire virtues to win the race. For we all have vices and will resort to them if we do not respect the captain."

Jim asked, "But how does a captain become that kind of person?"

All eyes were on Nate, who was quiet for a few minutes before answering. "We're given opportunities to be that kind of person every day, and we take one action after another in every moment of choice. Choosing what we know is right, instead of choosing what we might want in the moment, makes all the difference. Otherwise, we break ourselves in two. Eventually the loss of honor erodes our confidence and we lose our ability to lead entirely. Captains who have lost their vessels wander on land and lose the freedom of the seas. When we choose greed, pride, vanity, or any of the vices, the credibility that's fundamental to leadership begins to break down. No one can follow those who don't know who they are and who continue to lose more of themselves in every action."

"But how do we know what to choose in every situation?" Kit was still interested in the gut instinct she relied on.

"You'll know you've chosen rightly when you're willing to pay the price of being committed to your convictions. The hard part is knowing who you are, claiming it fully and then choosing to support it through every small action you take."

"And how will I know," asked Jim, "If I'm turning down the wrong path?"

"You'll know by the extremes in yourself. Extremes indicate an ego that is broken and trying to heal with an extreme reaction in opposition to the injury. For example, those who have an excessive need to be admired by others are trying to heal from their inability to accept and love themselves. Their inability to be alone and at peace is a symptom that love is not inside. And worse, these extremes are addictive. If you give too much away trying to buy what you need, there will never be enough external approval to counter the lack of approval in yourself. Another example are those people who want control and power because of their inner experience of powerlessness. For those not given a sense of internal personal power growing up, fear of their own vulnerability may show up as abuses of power. Extremes such as domination, bullying, arrogance or superiority are actually powerlessness in disguise. From these extremes, you'll only succeed at leading the weak and broken, those who are also *half a person*." He paused and let that sink in. It was a lot to take in, he knew.

After a few minutes, Nate continued. "Personal vitality and willpower provide the integrity and confidence to take command of a crew. Would you come aboard with someone who's glib and nonchalant, who doesn't take the role of captain seriously? Or one who's an opportunist? Would you sail into a storm with a captain who is arrogant and merciless? No, most of us would not. To attract and inspire the strongest crew, those who choose to be their best, one must set an example of personal will and self-leadership. This happens when captains know their unique *Tilt* but also know what it means to be whole, so they're able to regulate extremes that would otherwise take them astray. They respect the *Tilts* of others while requiring them to have good character, too. These are captains of the ships everyone wants to crew."

"What do you mean by a person's *Tilt*, Nate?" asked Kit. "Do you mean their personality and style preferences?"

"Exactly Kit, you're right. All of us have a set of gifts and strengths that make us excellent at certain roles. Knowing what those are requires us to know ourselves and be honest about the limitations of our preferences so we know when to call on others to contribute. Yet, the call to leadership requires more out of a person than a role on the crew does. A captain has to be capable of filling in for anyone on-board. There is a higher standard expected to be accepted as captain and one must recognize that more intentional self-mastery is required when you are responsible for the many."

There was a brief silence, and then Jean Claude said, "This is why I wanted to race the Whitbread with you, Nate. To be on a team with a great shot at winning, yet with a reputation for winning with grace. No one wants to go into a challenge with a weak captain. And speaking of the Whitbread, Nate, will you tell us about navigating storms?"

"Ah, and the storms do come, eh mate? When a storm is inevitable," said Nate, "the focus must first be on stability, on preparation, planning and building the relationships of the team. The captain must be strict about what keeps the crew from harm. Nowhere is this more important than at sea. Crew members who accept that rules of safety are there to protect them, and who are accountable to those rules, will be at their most creative when dealing with the surprises that inevitably arise. The captain who wants to reach a destination healthy and well cannot ignore stability or consistency."

Kit said, "This seems so obvious when you're talking about being in a boat on the ocean, but I'm thinking about how many clients I've had who ignore their responsibilities in favor of expedience. I wish they'd think about leadership this way. It would make things a lot easier in corporate storms! Seriously, I'm hearing from Nate that all crew members are important and their safety and well-being are his utmost concern. If we cared about the members of our teams in companies more, maybe they'd be more responsible and contribute to the mission with more conviction."

"Good point," agreed Jim. "I think if my leader showed he cared about me that much, I'd be more willing to trust my life into his hands. Trouble is, most of us don't know our leaders that well, so how would we know what they care about?"

"That's an important question, Jim," answered Nate. "You'll know what leaders care about when they share a vision for where they want to go in a way that excites you, too, and they also show their confidence in you to help achieve that vision. If a captain doesn't communicate this, why would anyone sign up for the voyage? Right, J.C.?" He looked over at his former crew member.

"Exactly. Had Nate not communicated his desire to circumnavigate the world in record time with confidence and conviction, I would not have signed up. Nate had a highly credible reputation in sailing circles. Most of the crew wanted the challenge of the journey, but we also wanted to experience a great leader. Nate demonstrated what he calls *Around the World to True Tilt* performance. True Tilt performance means everyone has to go East, West, North and South going full circle and becoming well-rounded and whole in order to be effective. A 360-degree circumnavigation gives them the experience to respond to all of the complex problems that can arise in such a dynamic environment. And yet, they also keep their focus on the destination and are the pacesetter for the crew to keep moving forward to the goal. Like a compass rose on a map that shows them true north. Once they have mastered the skills required for all possible directions, they can determine the perfect tilt for the conditions. This perfect tilt does not always coincide with what they personally do best, but they tilt that way because it is the best tilt for the situation. Then when they come back to their natural preference, their preferred tilt, they can be themselves with ease and confidence. They have confidence that comes from appreciating all sides to a situation and have the skills for any direction. They are true and balanced but uniquely their own person. This is when they become a blessing to the crew and the most creative contributor."

Addie asked "What's a compass rose, J.C.?"

"A compass rose is an ornate figure on almost all nautical maps, to orient the map to true north, east, west and south. It's an anchoring point for true direction. The meaning here is that leaders who are whole are able to navigate smoothly, considering all four directions at once. They're able to predict the True Tilt for external conditions. It's just Nate's way of saying we have to develop a capacity for balance in four specific areas and to know when to use each of them ~ in leadership those four qualities are Wisdom, Humanity, Courage and Resilience or more simply *Head, Heart, Gut* and *Spirit*. I learned this from my ancestor who wrote these things in her diary about the requirements of command at sea. And I could tell Nate had all four of these qualities."

Ian jumped in. "Hey J.C., I'm curious. In what ways did Nate exemplify those four qualities? You know he isn't going to talk about himself."

"Yeah, that's for sure. Nate, do you mind?" J.C. asked.

Reluctantly Nate agreed, but turned his gaze out to sea as if he wanted to focus elsewhere. It was clear to the others he wasn't interested in being in the spotlight or flattered unnecessarily. He always gave credit to his crews and yet he also knew that being a strong leader is not easy and takes personal thought and commitment, so he acquiesced by being silent.

Jean Claude began, "First, Nate had the knowledge and experience from his background with years of sailing experience to draw from~ *Wisdom*. He wasn't just smart, he had demonstrated consistently good judgment." "Second, he is compassionate and understands how to build esprit de corps, which let us know he had our best interests at heart and we could contribute our best to grow from the experience. We could make mistakes, as long as we learned from them quickly and didn't repeat them ~ *Humanity*. Third, he was known for his strong desire and will to win, so we could trust his personal conviction would be in it to give us persistent momentum through holding every one of us accountable to personal integrity~ *Courage*. Lastly, he'd applied creative solutions in tough spots in previous races, so he had the intelligence to lead creatively in complex dynamics ~ *Resilience*. He's very good at asking for input from the crew to inform him for optimum decision-making and then he was willing to put himself on the line and lead where he stands. It was the most exciting and challenging experience of my life to be on that crew and win that race, and it was a privilege to experience that kind of leadership. Nate has his leanings but he's balanced in all four aspects of leadership. He calls it managing your polarities. " J.C.'s eyes shone with admiration.

Nate looked back at Jean Claude with equal respect. "Well, that part actually came from your wise old ancestor Jean Claude. He taught me a lot on that trip as well. That's one reason we're here together."

Jean Claude chimed in, "Well, that's true. We had many long discussions about this on our voyage. From the diary, I learned that if a Captain overused his or her strengths and virtues to an extreme, then mutiny is possible. She observed that it is human nature for us to notice when someone in authority is over-tilting and their personality preferences are too extreme. The natural response is that some informal leader will rise in power and try to balance the extreme with an opposite stance. Then attempt to build a faction of support. This results in an emotionally divided crew, so the Captain has lost full respect and following. Mutiny can then happen in a crisis, putting the whole crew in danger. For example, if a Captain has too much compassion and overuses the virtues of *Humanity*, someone will smell weakness and pose a polar opposite position and build a faction that supports the virtues in *Courage*. Or the opposite can happen and the leader is too extreme in Courage, becoming overly arrogant and certain they are always right. The response will be a faction from those who want to balance it with virtues in *Humanity* like Trust and Consideration. There are similar issues in balancing *Wisdom* and *Resilience*. The key is balance in the leader, so that the power remains in balance for unity. If everyone respects the Captain, then they will work together as a team. If precious energy gets used up in power dynamics, then they lose focus on the work they have to accomplish together and risks arise."

Kit's ears perked up at the mention of Trust and Consideration in the same sentence. *Those were the two people I met. I wonder if they were "guides" trying to help me, like Ian had explained.* She felt a little guilty pang for some reason. Maybe she was over-tilting in Courage. She would have to ask Jean Claude about this later.

Addie wanted this moment to last a little longer, to let what she was hearing sink in. It wasn't a simple formula, but then she wasn't a fan of the quick fix. *Secret formulas that let you cheat the hard work of discipline don't get you anywhere.* She'd learned this and taught it to her team back home. Balance was how they had won the award in fact, so this theory rang true to her gut instinct. Now she remembered her childhood idealization of the heroine Dagny Taggart in

Atlas Shrugged, and realized the lack of balance in Dagny's perspective. *Her character glorified Courage and Wisdom and vilified Humanity and Resilience by only focusing on their extremes, despising people she saw as chameleon-like, weakened by the extremes of compassion that lead to permissiveness. Or despising the trait of optimistic idealism and trivializing it as blind faith that has no basis in fact. Her heroine could only see the vices of being over-tilted in people like her brother, so she entirely missed the gifts of the Humanity and Resilience perspectives in a balanced form and dismissed them as evil, seeing only the overdeveloped traits. Her mind raced with the possibilities of the new insight! Dagny had been close, but no cigar! What she'd missed was the importance of balance through embracing polar aspects.* Fascinated by the concept of balancing all four qualities of wholeness, Addie asked, "Nate, tell us how to prevent obstacles from causing us to go adrift. How can we know how to stay in the sweet spot, in flow, what you call 'True Tilt' in sailing?"

"Hmm, another good one, Addie. Our biggest obstacle is the distortion of reality when our own extremes cause us to heel over too far beyond the balanced tilt. As with a boat, when we lean too far, we lose balance and capsize. Pretty soon, if we're not aware and conscientious, we can tilt into trouble because we're not adjusting to the changing wind and conditions." Jim acknowledged this point with a nod of admission.

Nate continued, "For example, notice that while we're talking Ian continues to consider the dynamic environment, checking the instruments for wind direction, depth, currents, weather and other boats that may be in our path. He's changed out sails to take advantage of the optimum wind capture for the conditions. He's adjusted the rudder to change direction slightly as we move around shoals, obstacles, other boats. And he's kept his eyes on the telltales and adjusted the trim on the sail at least a dozen times today, to be sure the sails are at maximum efficiency. He's had his ear tuned to the radio for local weather report changes and he's checked the weather-fax twice for large-scale updates to the major weather patterns. He hasn't taken his eyes off of his duties once, unless he tagged someone else in. He's constantly aware of the environment around him and getting feedback. He's asked J.C. to double-check the GPS behind him and asked my opinion of the best plan to get there. He's not insecure, so he doesn't mind asking and he doesn't mind adjusting his course when he has new information. The best preventive measures for avoiding obstacles, Addie, are attending carefully to one's duties and strategically problem-solving as needed. Preparation and attention require personal will and responsibility. And all the while you've been enjoying the journey, so maybe you haven't noticed the small things. I've been watching, too, and am ready for anything. Accidents can happen even in good weather!" Nate smiled and winked at Ian. They'd had a problem on a recent trip when they forgot to put a preventer on the boom in case of a gybe. The boom had slammed to the other side of the boat when the wind switched and a shackle had broken causing all kinds of chaos on an otherwise easy sail.

"One more comment," he added. "And this may be the most important thing I've said so far. Crews reach their goals if all are fully conscious of their impact on others and interact with integrity. This requires a level of maturity that must be held in place by the captain as the highest example of what's required. When you take the helm, you must take seriously that you have more responsibility and risk than a member of the crew. Nonchalance, indifference, arrogance, recklessness and lack of self-reflection or regulation are deal breakers. If so-called leaders demonstrate any of these characteristics, or their vices are more prominent than their virtues, then do not put them in charge of other human beings or the ship will sink."

"Vices? Do you mean evil?" asked Jim.

"Vices are something we are all susceptible to, Jim, but we all have a conscience that will keep us in check. Evil is very extreme in that no conscience exists at all and you will know you have encountered evil when you look into the dead eyes of someone who is truly evil. Most of us will never encounter that kind of extreme, hopefully. Evil happens with those who have no capacity at all for self-reflection or regard for impact, so they really have no conscience. Without capacity for moral reasoning, they simply should not be put in charge. Of course it happens. But those leaders will eventually be incapacitated like Hitler was. Their ability to intimidate can delay the exposure of their flaws, but you can trust it will eventually happen. They may be leading a mission that's self-serving, but their vices will eventually render their mission unsustainable. If you have this kind of leader and don't find your voice and courage to challenge it, you will eventually sink with the ship. The question is, are you on the right ship, on the right voyage? It's as simple as that. But it takes integrity to choose your values over the short-term rewards of a ship on a mission of piracy. That's different than being on a vessel with a leader who simply has vices and is willing to acknowledge and work on them.

"Doesn't this call into question the need to respect authority?" asked Jim. "When do you choose integrity and when do you go along with authority if you don't agree with the direction? " All eyes were on Nate, indicating that this was an answer none of them wanted to miss.

"Everyone who signs on as crew and shares the booty must accept the captain's authority. A ship, with a good mission or a faulty mission, eventually sinks when mutiny is afoot. This is also why it's so important not to join or stay on a crew with the wrong person at the helm. If your values do not align with the captain's, you're on a mission that is not in your True Tilt. Your own moral compass will give you signs that this is the case. Then you have a choice. If you don't have strength of character to hold yourself and others accountable to good values, you may eventually start taking on the vices of those around you."

"And what about confidence? Doesn't that help?" asked Kit. "Aren't some people born more confident and driven than others?" She was certain she'd been born a leader and naturally took charge of almost every situation. She believed weakness was also something you were born with. And weakness meant you were not cut out for the job.

"That question has plagued philosophers through the ages, Kit. I think you're referring to what I might call the Heroes, or Leaders of Courage and Justice, born with personalities predisposed to tenacity, confidence and risk-taking. They start out as the Warriors and transcend into the Heroes when they learn the lesson of integrity. That's one kind of leader. But leadership, by definition, means you influence others to follow, and there are other ways to lead. The Wanderers transcend into the Seekers, or Leaders of Hope and Ideas, painting a creative picture of the future. When they learn that the grass is not greener on the other side, they learn to focus and plant roots so they can invent and create what the rest of us would never think of. There are also the Rulers, or Leaders of Truth who transcend into the Sages. They are the builders of rules and systems that help us execute our plans and be safe while doing so. When they learn the lesson of faith, they begin to let go and trust that they will be safe from harm even when they take risks. They are the great historians who advance human knowledge and most of our privileges are built on the backs of their work. And then there are the Helpers who become the Healers, and are the Leaders of Service and Care for others. When they learn that they must first take care of themselves in order to care for others in the best possible way, they become the healers of our sorrows and are able to lighten the world's burdens.

The finest leaders of all, though rare, are those whose creative capacity is limitless because they have become lifelong learners and are all four: the Seeker, the Hero, the Sage *and* the Healer join to become the Creator. So, Kit, we are all unborn leaders when we begin our journey. And we can all become leaders when we find out who we are and what we've been designed to do. If we take the mantle of leadership sincerely and commit to a lifelong journey of growth, we will develop *all four* aspects of leadership and transcend to higher levels of consciousness and creativity, contributing and giving back a legacy to the world we leave behind. Many do not take this divergent path because it requires too much of them."

Nate paused for his listeners to absorb all he'd said. He needed this team to be ready for the challenge ahead of them. There was much at stake and he would soon find out what each of them was made of. As the sun began to set and the sky filled with the familiar Caribbean pinks and purples, he said "One more question, and then off to our bunks so we're ready tomorrow. J.C. and I are on watch tonight and need a few winks before we come back up top."

"I have so many people on my team who want to be leaders," said Addie. "How do I help them know when they're ready?"

"Ah, a good question for late-night pondering," replied Nate. "You know you're a leader when a persistent internal voice rises within you. When you hear it, and you commit to it, the courage of conviction gives you a mission to fulfill. One that's yours alone, that no one else is as uniquely prepared to accomplish. It happens when you know you *must* do something, and if you don't, your heart will break for what will be missing if you don't. You decide to give the world a new creative product, or prevent some problem, or solve another, or care for those who cannot care for themselves. True leaders will give their life efforts for a great cause and offer a path that others will follow. Woe be to those Seekers who are called and do not accept the challenge that only they can fulfill. They are the hopeless and the lost, walking through life in a trance, on a journey that will take them to the wrong port, and they won't know this until they're old and it's too late."

Nate stretched his arms and yawned. "Off to my bunk for a rest! It's been a pleasure and great honor to know each of you and be part of your quest for answers. I see that all of you are Seekers who have accepted the challenge, and that does my old heart some good. I'm grateful to you for that." He lifted his large frame with an ease that spoke of comfort with his surroundings and disappeared quickly down the companionway.

Addie said goodnight and wandered up to the bow to lie down on the deck next to Barnacle. The teak planks beneath her back still held the sun's warmth, and she stretched out to contemplate Nate's words while scratching the scraggly hound behind the ears. Barnacle licked her salty arm with a long, appreciative kiss and snuggled up by her side. The black sky of the Caribbean, in such contrast to the countless stars, took her breath away.

Chapter 26

TCMP News Release
Tobago Cays Marine Park
Volume 2-Special Announcement

Since the establishment of the Tabago Cays Marine Park in 1997, the local government of St. Vincent and the Grenadines has struggled with how to effectively manage the protection and conservation of one of the most important world-class resources, the third largest natural reef in the world. Board problems, legal discrepancies and lack of effective management caused the French government to withdraw funding in 2001. Several studies have been conducted to determine the best approach to managing the resource, but the park manager has described slow progress with implementation up to this time. Despite the importance of this natural resource, there is growing evidence that the ecosystem is being affected by non-sustainable use and both natural and man-made use impacts. Reef bleaching and white band disease are concerning and threaten the entire ecosystem, including the survival of many species of animals impacted by the onslaught of increased development and tourism impacts.

In May of 2009, it was announced that the Government was considering a proposal for the day-to-day management of Tabago Cays Marine Park, to be contracted to a Caribbean hotel chain called Island Palm Resorts, recently purchased by US-based hotel developer Pyramid International, which plans to build a resort on the last privately-owned island of the lower Caribbean, in Mayreau. Also included in their plan is to build resorts on Bequia and Grenada, as well as a string of other islands in the Windwards. Concerns about the impact of the resort planned for Bequia include the location near the Old Hegg Turtle Sanctuary, where Brother King has spent his life trying to preserve endangered Caribbean Sea turtles. The company has promised to provide the necessary resources and management to the TCMP and to other causes like that of Brother King, but many feel the motives of the company are suspect.

A coalition of local citizens objects to the proposal, citing concern about the proposer's prioritization of profitability over biodiversity conservation. The plan would have seen several structures erected on parts of the islands that have never been developed. The concept of handing a prized national asset over to a foreign and private company caused a public outcry last month. The company is an unknown to the Caribbean officials and has made a move to purchase another local chain that includes existing hotels in Barbados, St. Lucia, St. Croix and Dominica. Little is known of the hotel operator's management policies and whether they would be concerned with the interests of local resources and citizens.

More Recent NEWS: A local NGO, the Mayreau Environmental Development Organization (MEDO) has submitted a counter-proposal to the Marine Parks Board. This proposal is currently under Board evaluation.

Concerned parties should write to the Coalition for the Preservation of Tabago Cays National Preserve. Submit to admn@CTNP.com.

Chapter 27

Another gorgeous day of sailing quieted the crew. Everyone stepped into the rhythm of pleasure that only a full experience of nature can provide. The following seas gracefully pushed the *True Tilt* forward faster as she surfed down the mountainous ocean waves, traveling at nearly ten knots. Ian was ecstatic about the time they were making. The eighteen knots of apparent wind were just enough to provide a straight shot to the island with no tacking needed.

As the evening approached and a fabulous meal prepared by Jean Claude and Addie filled their bellies, the crew settled into another evening of discussion.

"Jean Claude, you've outdone yourself again," Ian said. "Chicken Roti is one of my favorite treats, so I for one am highly appreciative you resumed the galley duties tonight and taught Addie this delectable dish."

"Here, here," said Jim, who looked more and more relaxed as the voyage continued. "I'm hoping for more sailing lore from you experienced sailors. I dreamt about sailing and tilting in the wind, and I have a couple more questions that woke me up early this morning."

"Me too," Addie joined in. "There's so much wisdom in your stories I could barely sleep last night."

Kit asked, "Maybe Nate can help us apply what we're learning here to the mission we're on?"

"Soon enough, soon enough, Kit," said Ian. "You'll get your assignment in the morning." He knew Kit's preference for results and guessed she was struggling more than the others, not knowing all the details. *The strongest swimmer is often the last one to climb on the boat. Natural confidence is a good thing, unless the depth isn't there. Can she manage her impatience when she needs to do her homework or question herself willingly? We'll find out, soon enough.*

Nate turned to Jim. "What questions are on your mind?"

"If you know you've gone adrift and your extremes have gotten you off track, how do you get back into the right tilt for you?" His own personal decisions were on his mind.

"A courageous question, Jim. All of us go astray at times when we're not being present with ourselves and are just reacting to life or going through the motions without awareness. Before we know it, we've gone out on a limb, experienced the potential of our vices and don't know how to get back. The good news is that it's never too late. If we're aware we're off course, we're halfway there. Then we have to think about who we want to be as we go forward, and choose to take the first step in that direction. Then the next. And the next. If instead we whine, complain, excuse, defend, blame, rationalize or otherwise deflect the awareness that we're off course, we'll keep going farther out on the limb. Anything that distracts us from being in congruence with our integrity and honor takes us down the wrong path. We can't control what others do; we can't control the weather or the struggles that come our way. But we can control how we respond. We have the power to choose a life of meaning and purpose, a life that's good and leaves the world a better place. Or we can choose to increase ourselves through the losses of others. Takers instead of contributors. And our choices add up to the total sum of what we become. So the question is, always, who are you when no one is watching? Who are you to those who count on you or have trusted you with something precious to them?"

"But if my personality causes me problems and I can't help it because that's what I was born with, what then?" asked Jim, thinking his charming ways had caused him more trouble than good.

"We're not just a personality, Jim," said Ian. "We do have certain predispositions when we're born, and we learn to capitalize on those tendencies as we cope with our environment. So, the personality becomes a strategy for survival. But we're so much more than that. We also have will and soul and spirit. Our will is how we exercise control over our personality to do what's good for our relationships. Our soul grounds us in our truth and spirit whispers our purpose to us, if we listen. We have the ability to observe what we're thinking so we can evaluate it for effectiveness. And we have choice – the ultimate freedom. Even when everything we love is taken from us, we still have the choice of how we'll think about and respond to it. With choice, we can have purpose and meaning."

"Ian's point is very good," said Nate. "Our purpose changes over the span of our lives. We start with a hunger for learning and are like sponges taking it all in. Then we develop experience and focus to build our lives. We build through our work and taking care of our families, which are precious gifts entrusted to us. Eventually, when our work is done, we shift to a different kind of contribution. We begin to care about the world our children will inherit and yearn to improve it through wisdom we've gained. But all throughout life, we cannot lead without purpose. As purpose changes, so does our responsibility for who we become. Jim, you can choose your purpose in the very next thing you do today. You don't get to be a leader simply because someone gave you a title. You become a leader because of who you are and what you influence."

Addie had one final question and then she planned to crash for the night. Yawning, she asked, "Nate, why is it that good people act so badly when they're on a team with a bad leader? What is it that can make them go south so quickly?"

"That's a tough one, Addie. But one that deserves an answer because a lot of us are that way. There are rare souls who are so grounded they can remain in integrity no matter how bad things become. They're the fortunate ones whose parents were wise and gave them a solid set of beliefs and discipline. The rest of us cannot stay as strong in a turbulent environment, but we know lack of integrity when we see it. We polarize to extremes and either try to escape what's wrong or rebel against it. As soon as we notice, we must catch ourselves and exercise the composure that comes from personal integrity, so we can trust in what's right to win in the end. Therefore, temperance is the foundation of leadership because when the leader is calm, everyone can be calm, the first step to finding balance again. In sailing, we say you must first find balance, and then you can capture the wind in the Tilt. But True Tilt will not happen without the weight of the ballast to balance it."

Ian stood up and began gathering the last of the dinner plates. "Off to your bunks now, everyone except Nate and Jean Claude. You need to be rested and you've enough to consider before we begin our task tomorrow. We rise at sun-up and the briefing will start at 6 a.m. sharp." His tone gave no opening for argument.

Chapter 28

As the sun rose over the horizon, the crew of the *True Tilt* pulled in her sails and prepared to drop anchor in the bright blue waters of Saltwhistle Bay. Addie closed out her 3 – 6 a.m. shift at the helm, entering latitude, longitude and weather into the ship's logbook, elated that she'd easily awakened at 2:45 for her shift and hadn't been the least bit nauseated. Kit placed the sails in their covers with her usual brisk agility. Jim was at the nav station telling J.C., now at the helm, the best approach to the channel into Saltwhistle Bay.

Addie marveled at how far they'd come as a team in such a short time. *Mastering a challenge together, especially when life-threatening, connects people emotionally in a way that doesn't often happen in business.* Reflecting on Nate's words, she thought how none of them had for one minute questioned Ian's authority as a leader. Of course he was the one with the experience and credibility in this setting, but he carried himself with authority and also brought out their best. *Then, when he was in trouble, we pulled together to save our leader and solve the challenge.* She was forming theories based on observing leadership, not in an academic way but embodied in life-and-death experience. Except for her strong desire to return to Emma, she no longer wanted to go back to her old, superficial life. She was about to embark on a whole new path, and felt open to what this might bring.

Jim motioned for her to join him and Kit on the bow. Ian and the others were busy talking in the captain's quarters, so she cajoled Barnacle into going forward with her. *The ole rascal has inched his way into my heart.* She hadn't had a dog in years and was surprised by his intelligence and emotional capacity. Their connection had grown swiftly.

"Addie," Kit whispered. "Jim just told me the map is missing from his cabin, and he thinks he saw Jean Claude with it in the cockpit on the midnight shift. We've got to get it back and find whatever it points to before anyone else does. These signs were intended for us, I know it! Make sure you keep your compass with you at all times. I need to get my key back from Ian, too. When we have all the pieces together, we can find a few hours to ourselves and let them do whatever Nate has them working on. Someone local can tell us where the cave is."

Jim said, "What if we're supposed to be helping Nate, Ian and J.C. on their project, and this is not about us at all?"

"Yeah, Kit," Addie agreed. "I think we should tell Ian about these clues. Maybe they have something to do with the project. And Nate told us he needed us to help him. What if the compass is part of the puzzle?"

"No way!" Kit was vehement. "We're being given the chance of a lifetime. Who cares about a bunch of turtles and a reef? We might find an ancient treasure that's been lost for decades. Did you hear Jean Claude talking about his privateer ancestor? Maybe she buried something in that cave. We have a compass, a map and a key! What more do you need to tell you there's something at the end of that big red X on the map? We have to get them back when Ian isn't looking." Kit laid out the plan she'd been obsessing over. She wanted to find what was in that cave and get the heck home to Dallas for Sebastian's project. She was worried he might even turn it down if she didn't go back soon, but she had to quickly pursue this trip's opportunistic angle. *Sebastian probably set this whole thing up to test my creativity and persuasion skills. I know who's a leader and who's not. Jim and Addie haven't made one move that looks like leadership since I've met them.*

Addie fingered a lock of her hair, spun it in quick circles around her finger, tied it into a knot and tucked it behind her ear. She was caught up in Kit's excitement, but something was holding her back.

Just then Jim said, "Okay, let's go for it, Kit, but you're on your own if you can't get the map and key back from Ian. I'm not going to have any part of sneaking into his cabin." Jim had decided to start paying attention to making small choices for integrity and he wasn't about to make this mistake.

"No problem!" said Kit, "I am ON IT. Once I've found them, all we have to do is find a couple of hours and get some local information."

Addie found herself thinking that Kit was in an extreme and playing with a Vice. *Hadn't she been listening yesterday, or didn't she get it?*

Chapter 29

Nate and Ian came up the companionway and said everyone would head to the Black Baron Tavern to meet the governor of St. Vincent, who would debrief them before the next day's meeting with the local government. As Ian had explained that morning, they were to be consultants on the project.

"Let's head in and grab some lunch," said Nate. "There's a semi-private room at the Black Baron." Barnacle was pacing back and forth, panting in anticipation.

Kit scowled, her plan to sneak into Ian's cabin foiled. Reluctantly she joined the others, lowered herself into the *Near Tilt* and tried to feign interest as Nate continued telling them about troubles managing the local conservation efforts.

Nate had lived on Mayreau for the past four years and had grown to love the villagers of this small utopia. "They're completely self-sufficient and harmonious – no police, no violence, no government save three justices of the peace. Not even any money changing hands except for local tourists' spending at the small resort in Saltwhistle Bay. The money made there goes into the fund that supports community needs, like the generator that brought electricity to the island two years ago. Everything the local population needs to sustain itself is grown and harvested locally. Their water source is rain, caught in three cisterns on the north side of the island. The only trades are fishing, farming and tourism. Mayreau is the only privately-owned island left in the lower Caribbean, independent of a larger governing country. The islanders are a mixture of American Indian, Carib, French and African. The French settled here in the 1700's, and the land was eventually purchased by one family. The matron owner, a woman called Miss Rose, has allowed people to build wherever they liked and half the harvested crops were shared with her family for many years. For decades, their sustenance has been provided by salt mined from the North Bay and cotton farmed in the fields."

Nate's voice was animated as he made the case for helping locals solve the problems they faced. He'd bought a portion of land from the family, who welcomed the skills he and his wife Kate brought to help protect their fishing livelihood. Fishing and yachting by tourists from all over the world were deteriorating their natural resources and threatening to disrupt the local population's sustainability. The development of hotels and golf courses had catalyzed a drastic bout of reef bleaching caused by the runoff of pesticides and fertilizers that were killing reef life. And hundreds of yachts were discharging waste and rubbish in the once pristine waters, a fragile home for thousands of species now on the brink of extinction.

Up to now, Addie had no concept of a place like this, where children wore no shoes and people had no money, yet lived in a glorious haven of natural beauty. Nate's passion for this part of the world was emotionally compelling in a way she hadn't known in her materially-focused existence. Her heart ached from the human potential to harm one another, even if it was sometimes unintentional. It struck her that people's capacity to ignore the impact of their choices was both remarkable and sad. *How could we know human advancement and development would have such a wide-reaching impact on so many species of life?* Ian, as a marine biologist, held expanses of knowledge she knew nothing about, a world of science completely out of her realm of experience. But she'd heard it said the story of an animal harmed would make even the most callous weep with compassion. *What a strange back door to the human heart.*

As they crossed the bay in the *Near Tilt* Nate said, "The latest news is that a Caribbean hotel chain, Island Palm Resorts, recently acquired by Pyramid International, has offered to govern the conservatory of the lower islands, including all those close to the great reef. Headquartered in Miami, the company has offered resources to fund the management of the conservatory, but only if they can build more resorts on Mayreau. Because the island of

Mayreau is fairly small, this means the Old Wall Village would have to be relocated to the less desirable north shores, which would be devastating to the local population. Though the villagers have an alliance with the Grenadines' governing body, which protects the resources they depend on, they don't have the money to defend themselves against a majority vote in this matter if they want to continue to enjoy the protection of its government benefits. In short, they have a major dilemma."

Ian's spoke with grave concern. "They're stuck in the middle of a no-win scenario. The Grenadines officials want them to give in, to benefit all the islands, but they'll suffer overwhelming change to the life they've known for centuries. There's also a faction of activists trying to block the hotel, casino and golf course from being built. These people are suspicious of the hotel chain's motives because they've seen the damage from other hotels developed in the Windwards and they don't know the motives of the new owner, Pyramid. I'm trying to educate all of them about the additional damage the development could cause to marine life, hoping we can be creative about how we move forward. A new resort in Bequia may also mean the end of the turtle sanctuary."

The six of them climbed out of the *Near Tilt*, tied the painter to the dock and walked up the beach to the private room in the tavern. Ian spread papers out on the wooden table and continued the briefing for the meeting that would come later that day.

Addie's thoughts suddenly came to attention. The name of the hotel chain Nate had mentioned was familiar. *Wasn't that company part of the acquisition by the private equity firm, the last transaction underway and included in the same purchase as my company?* When she got a chance, she'd have to call the office and find out what she could about this.

Ian was now describing the history of sport fishing that had been popularized in the last few decades by author Ernest Hemingway. "...which contributes to some degree, but mostly it's the dramatically increased commercial demand for fresh fish made possible by overnight delivery, and we've seen big changes in the life cycle of marine life over the last fifty years. There's now record-breaking demand for fresh fish in our diets, and extreme overfishing has depleted the ocean worldwide, interrupting the normal food chain and threatening thousands of species. It's a global problem that's escalating every year. The largest predatory fish are exploited until they're depleted and then commercial fisheries move to the next best species. The U.N. Food and Agriculture Organization reports that 62% of fish stocks are exploited today, with 7% fully depleted and another 35% moderately depleted. This presents two serious global problems. First, we're not only losing species. Entire ecosystems of our oceans are under tremendous stress and at risk of collapse, if we don't reverse the exploitation. Economically, we're also at risk of losing valuable food sources, as well as industries that depend on the ecosystem's resources. This creates local problems like the ones we'll talk about at today's meeting."

Nate said, "Ian, tell them about the cod industry in Canada. That was enlightening to me."

"Nate's referring to one of the best examples of how this problem will end for so many local communities. The cod industry in Newfoundland, Canada, came to a screeching halt in 1992 when the cod didn't show up one year. Mismanagement, overfishing and unnecessary decay of an ecosystem lost 40,000 people their livelihood. Now, they survive by harvesting crab that was previously considered a nuisance to the cod industry. Unless they've learned their lesson, they'll deplete that next level in the chain, too. According to a scientist I read recently, we could end up with 'little horrible things no one wants to eat and a sea dominated by plankton.' I think he nailed it. Unless we solve these problems locally and then work globally to report the facts, we're headed for implications that will change the world our children inherit." Ian stopped to let the bigger picture sink in.

Nate added, "The local people used to depend on fishing as their top industry. With tourism having such a negative impact, they're in a mess. The local governing body of the conservatory has struggled with lack of focus and resources. The resources they did have were recently taken away because of inconsistency and ineffectiveness of board leadership. They're left with few choices and divided on this matter locally, tempted to give away their power to the hotel chain that promises to save them. Your task as consultants is to help find a solution that gives them both leadership and sustainability of that leadership. Each of you has specialized skills that can help diagnose and empower them with knowledge they may not have without you. You're here for their benefit and for your own learning."

"Kit," Ian said, "you're an expert at leadership development and mediating cultural differences. Addie, you're an accomplished leader in the hotel industry and will understand the hotel chain's motives. Jim, you're experienced in creative social networking and public relations, which will help unify everyone. Jean Claude can enlighten us about the legal issues. As a marine biologist, I can ignite concern for the long-term impact of their choice. And Nate is here because he cares about the people of Mayreau and what's at stake for them. He's been a world traveler and leader, but he's retired and no longer wishes to be in charge. He and Kate had hoped to live their last years simply, undisturbed by the external world. He's happy to provide what wisdom he can, and is here to support you behind the scenes, but doesn't want a public role in the solution. It's time for future leaders to step up and take on the task of leadership."

Jim asked, "Do you have any data on the various voices of opinion in the region?"

Ian replied, "All the data you'll need is here. It will take the afternoon to digest it and I suggest we first hear from the governor of St. Vincent, who's the current leader in charge of the lower islands. This will be your chance to understand local perceptions. You can dive into the details and history this afternoon."

"I'm with Jim," Kit said. "We need to understand their leadership history, and I have questions about resource availability, too."

"I'll need to see the legal documents in question," J.C. added, "including the board documents, and Addie, if you can get any information on the hotel acquisition plans that would help a lot."

Addie asked, "What time do we begin this morning? I need to make some calls about the hotel company in question, and would like to do that before we meet if there's time."

Nate looked at Jean Claude and smiled. "I think we have a team on this challenge." The relief he felt was reflected in his otherwise tired eyes and face.

"Seems so," Jean Claude replied with a smile in return. "Trust us to put our minds together, Nate. We'll see what we can do."

With that, Nate leaned back in his chair and went into listening mode for the remainder of the day, while the team began work on what they did best. Whatever the outcome, he knew he would accept it. The world was escalating to an overwhelming level of complexity. His leadership had been in the wide-open space of nature. He and Kate had come here to escape the insanity of leaders without character who ignored their impact on the environment he knew so well from his voyages. The changes had been noticeable to him because of his world travels over the last few decades. Then the problems had penetrated the small utopia of Mayreau, too. His heart ached for the future. But as he watched the bright faces of these young leaders, he felt a spark of hope.

Chapter 30

Seth's plan was in danger of falling apart. His lawyers were scrambling, spending hundreds of thousands of dollars trying to save it. Dellwood's death had seemed a stroke of good fortune at first, but Seth hadn't realized its impact on trying to close the complicated transaction. Moving the money he needed into the country from his sources in South America relied on a paper trail that had not been executed by the two remaining hotel chains, including the Island Palm Resorts in the Caribbean and Stanton Suites. The money from opium crops were to be laundered into his operation through Nicolai's hotel in Trinidad. Without it, he couldn't fund his share of Dellwood's private equity company and wouldn't have control. The Cavanaugh family had been a royal pain in the ass, thwarting all his attempts to resolve the situation. Dellwood's ridiculous sister, Reece, had been a particular thorn in his side for the last several weeks, as his attorneys tried every angle they could conjure up. Seth hadn't slept for weeks, his obsession with all the complex details taxing him beyond his limits. He was about to explode with rage. Everything he'd worked for the past ten years was going down the tubes within the space of three short weeks.

Then there was Nicolai, who hadn't yet managed to sneak away the map and the key. If Seth could get his hands on the jewels buried on that island, he could sell them on the black market and might have a prayer of coming up with the cash he needed. He couldn't count on it, though. Seth thought about the letter Nicolai had used to persuade Seth to fund him as owner of the Trinidad Hotel that would launder the secret stream of income. The letter had looked ancient, supposedly passed on for three centuries by the women in Nicolai's family. Until his mother died and his father got hold of it. Nicolai said his father, a drunk and a coward, had not pursued the lead to the cave in the lower Caribbean where the treasure lay. If the letter was authentic, some of the largest jewels in the world were hidden in that cave. The two of them were in alliance now, and the only ones who knew about the jewels. He was funding Nicolai's pursuit of the clues and, once the transaction was completed, would reward Nicolai with the power he craved – a role that would include doing the dirty work. Seth smiled as he thought about the plan. He couldn't let anything stop him. But the stress was almost unbearable. He picked up the phone to scream at one of the attorneys. That would make him feel better.

Chapter 31

Addie stepped out of the room to make some phone calls back to headquarters. David, her old boss and confidant, answered on the first ring. "Addie, I thought I told you to get on a plane and get back here!" His tone was exasperated.

"I know, I know," she replied. "I'm in the middle of a situation someone in the company volunteered me for, and I have to see it through. Am I in trouble?"

"No, I don't think so. It's just that I was asked to pull you in, and now they're looking at me like I can't get it done. Embarrassing, really, Addie. I'm looking like an idiot because I don't know where you are and why you aren't here. You're usually so cooperative. Can you get on a plane?"

"Well….*maybe*. I don't know. Maybe I should talk with Mark? I can call him from here and see what he needs. I put in for vacation and I have six weeks a year. I thought I could take three of them now."

"Addie, you know they don't mean for you to take vacation more than one week at a time. Good grief, woman, we can't afford for you to be gone that long, especially when you're out of email range. You're really taking some chances. But Leigh doesn't seem to be concerned. I was in a strategy meeting about the problems with the closing and when it came up that you were out of the country, she kind of smiled like she knew something. You sure are lucky the CEO's so fond of you. But don't forget, Mark's the one restructuring the team. You need to be here to defend your turf with the COO who really runs the show. Leigh gives him a lot of rope. I can only do so much now that I'm a lame duck, so to speak, until I go over to the gaming division."

"I know, David. That's a great promotion and I'm happy for you. Do you have to move?"

"Yeah, yeah, no big deal, done it a dozen times."

A possibility piqued Addie's interest and changed the direction of her thoughts. "Hey, David, can you give me Leigh's direct line?"

"You kidding? You're going to call the CEO right now?"

"I have a question only she can answer, that's all. Can you look it up?" Addie was excited.

"Sure, here it is." David gave her the number, then scolded her one more time for not playing politics the way she needed to if she wanted to keep her territory. "Don't forget, I *warned* you."

Hanging up, Addie made a few notes about what she'd say. She had an inkling Leigh had been the one to send her here, for personal development. And her mentor of the past year was going to get more than she bargained for. She'd always said Addie needed to show more courage. Now was the time. Picking up the phone to call Leigh was the easiest thing she'd done in a long time. She had a strong desire to say what she was feeling. It would go against the grain of popular opinion, but it needed to be said.

"Leigh Merriweather's office," she heard the executive assistant answer on the other end of the line.

"May I speak to Leigh? This is Addie Duke and it's important." "Sure, I think she was waiting for your call, Addie. Just a minute." *Waiting for my call? That's weird.* Within 30 seconds she heard a click on the line at the other end as Leigh picked up her office phone.

"Well, I've been looking forward to hearing from you, Addie," Leigh greeted one of her favorite protégées.

"So, it *was* you!" Addie replied, grinning from ear to ear. "You're the one who lured me off to this crazy development assignment, then?"

"Well, it's a bit more interesting than a development assignment, Addie, but yes, I'm the one who sent you off to the *True Tilt*. Have you figured out the lay of the land yet?"

"I've certainly experienced an altered perspective, if that's what you mean, Leigh. The whole world looks different to me now."

"As expected, then. I wanted your honest perspective. And I wanted to have a leader I can trust down there, figuring out what Seth is planning. I don't trust that man and I'm working around the clock to back out of this deal struck between Mike and Dellwood. For the life of me, I can't understand why mergers and acquisitions are so alluring. It's the greed, of course. The way the system is designed, it'll be a miracle if we have any honest CEOs left in this country by the turn of the decade. It was so easy for me to get seduced by the money we would have made on that transaction. To think I was going along with it! Dellwood is a convincing man and it seemed he'd keep our brands intact. Now that Seth is in charge, I'm certain the company as we know it will never be the same. He's brilliant on stage, and convincing to the masses with his mom and apple pie messages, but I can see straight through him. Don't ask me why, but I only see predatory opportunism in him – he's out for himself. All that warmth and love you see on stage disappears when you're alone with him." Leigh was being uncharacteristically open with Addie.

"Leigh, I'm so relieved to hear you say this. I was thinking of leaving the firm after this acquisition. The company I've been so proud of is changing. I just wasn't sure I could work in such a large company where people no longer matter. All the things that got me on that stage three weeks ago don't seem to matter anymore. I was actually calling to resign!"

"Wow, you really have changed, Addie. And now I know I can count on you to help me straighten out this mess. Are you in?" The CEO waited silently for her answer.

What Leigh had shared changed everything. Maybe there was hope. And if not, she could resign later. Right now she knew Leigh was counting on her and so was the team she had come to care about. She had to see this through. For herself, as well. She wanted to see this through.

"Of course, Leigh, you know I'm in. What's the plan?"

Chapter 32

Addie had left the small room, and all four of the men were leaning around the table engrossed in the conversation about the project. Kit, impatient, was half listening, while trying to think of a way to get back to the boat to find the map and key hidden in Ian's quarters. She'd watched how Ian fired up the motor on the *Near Tilt* and was confident she could operate it on her own. "Fellows, I'd like to take a walk and get some air. The meeting with the governor isn't for another hour and a half, so I thought I'd do a little incubating on this problem and maybe it will help me to come up with a creative solution. It's the way I like to do things. Do you mind?"

"OK," said Ian, "but be back at least fifteen minutes before noon so we can proceed with understanding the situation from their point of view. I think we all know what we're doing, but I'd like to confirm we're in alignment. You know your role, so if you're comfortable with that, we can manage the other aspects without you." Ian was a little annoyed, but trying to accommodate her needs.

"Good to go, then! I'll be back before you know it." Kit was out the door in a flash.

The heaviness of the Caribbean sun's heat took the wind out of her as she stepped onto the beach and headed for the dock where the *Near Tilt* was tied up. Sweat collected on her brow as she maneuvered into the small craft and fired up the motor, which was hot to the touch. Pulling up to the dock, motor idling, she loosened the painter and pushed away. She congratulated herself on paying extra for the polarized designer sunglasses she'd bought on her last trip to Tahiti. She could see the *True Tilt* clearly out in the bay beyond some two dozen other yachts, despite the sun's glare. She revved up the motor and let the small craft plane up into the air so she could run at full speed. Her experience boating at the lake years ago was coming in handy.

Kit boarded the *True Tilt* minutes later, climbing up the drop ladder and pulling herself up over the transom to the beautiful yacht's teak deck. She scurried into the cockpit and reached into the lazarette locker to the place she knew Ian kept the backup key in an envelope. He'd shown it to them as a precaution, in case one of them needed it at some point. She appreciated Ian's cautious nature and smiled to herself. *Some people never do a darned thing because they're so cautious. Not me! You have to take chances in this world to get ahead.*

Kit headed to the captain's quarters below deck and began searching for the map and the key. Rummaging through the lockers and under the mattress, she located several secret compartments behind and beneath the more obvious spaces. Under the mattress was a lid with an imbedded handle in its center. She lifted the lid and found what she was looking for. The map and the key were lying under his backpack. The generator that powered the air conditioning was turned off, and sweat was now pouring down between her breasts. The grueling heat was overwhelming. She returned to her cabin to find something to hide the items in, locating a large cloth bag she'd folded and stowed in her duffel in case she needed it. She placed the map and key inside, picked up the bag, closed the door to her cabin and turned to head back up the companionway. An instant of adrenaline rush shocked her body and she stopped cold in her tracks. Before her stood the most menacing-looking man she'd ever seen.

Black hair, black stubble on his face, cold black eyes, and a bad complexion. Nicolai grinned at the happy surprise he'd stumbled upon. Calling to the deck above, he summoned his companion to come do the dirty work. He motioned to the unfortunate redhead to pass him the bag and looked inside to make sure the contents were what he was here to find. Smiling with satisfaction, he stepped aside while Brutus tied up his prize. It was unfortunate for her to have been here when he arrived, but it seemed good fortune was smiling on him, finally. He'd have to contemplate the interesting options open to him, now that this redhead was in his possession. *Well done.*

Brutus tied Kit's hands behind her back and put duct tape over her mouth and eyes, stretching it all the way around her head, over her hair, and yanking it with pleasure. Kit's scream went unnoticed because he'd popped a cloth into her mouth before taping it shut. He pulled her up on deck and over to the Viking yacht Seth had chartered for Nicolai, taking a windbreaker from the foulie locker and draping it over her shoulders to avoid catching attention from other yachts in the bay. Luckily it was almost noon and none of the other yachties were on deck, due to the heat.

Another stroke of luck, Nicolai thought as he watched Brutus and his struggling cargo. *Seth will be pleased.*

He'd been following them all the way from Tortola and had yet to find the cabin unlocked. He didn't want to raise any suspicions by damaging the yacht, because he needed the advantage of time. The jewels were not going to be easy to find after 300 years. He needed every minute he could get on his side.

Kit's panic turned into rage and she pulled against the huge man shoving her aboard the large powerboat tied up next to the *True Tilt*'s transom. He yanked her on-board the Viking and guided her to the cabin below where he pushed her into a small room and threw her onto the bed. She tried to kick him as she landed, but he'd already backed away. She heard the cabin door slam and a click from outside. *He's locking me in.* Then she heard what sounded like a gun being loaded and placed on the table in the parlor. *What have I gotten myself into? The meeting at the tavern! Will they notice I'm gone? How foolish to not let anyone know what I was doing!* She heard the engine start up and the two men talking in deep, low tones. She couldn't quite tell what they were saying. One of them sounded like he was talking to someone else on the phone. She felt the boat moving, and guessed the big man was focused on the best path through the yachts out of the bay. The boat sped up and didn't stop racing at full speed for what felt like an hour. *They'll never find me now...*

Chapter 33

Seth had been brooding about Dellwood's untimely death for three weeks. His head pounded unmercifully from hours of obsessive thoughts as he tried to figure a way out of this complicated entanglement. *I hate the man.* Dellwood used to taunt him about his Ivy League education. Seth had devoted twenty years of his life to complete two law degrees, an MBA and a PhD in economics, and was still saddled with debts from educational loans. But no matter what credentials he piled up, he felt he needed more. And most of what he learned was forgotten because he had been after the grade instead of the mastery of the learning material. He retained only what is useful to his opportunistic habits. Dellwood, a self-made man worth billions by the time of his death, said what Seth lacked was street sense and basic decency. When he thought of this it made him furious.

Seth was on the brink of financial disaster and resented needing Dellwood, who said he put up with Seth's "highbrow ways" because it was what Wall Street said you should have for a CFO. Seth had the gift of oration and skills in creative accounting, yet Dellwood would minimize and dismiss him as if he were just an annoying necessity. Too many conversations ended with Seth fuming over how Dellwood underestimated him. His father had been the same way and the rage he felt as a consequence had propelled him through his education.

Dellwood's last words in the acquisition meeting reverberated through his mind. "Damn it Seth, don't you have a brain beneath that educated skull of yours? I am NOT going to make you the CEO. You'd run this company into the ground within a year with your superficial bullcrap. The way you get everyone all hyped up on your speeches is all smoke and mirrors, man! I wouldn't trust you with my left elbow. We don't have any intention of following through on the promises you're making and you know it. At least you could be honest and let them know most are going to be let go due to redundancies. Once this thing is over, I'm going to use you to break it up and sell off the assets, and then I'm going to wipe my hands clean. I wish I'd never let myself get caught up in the money machine. The most fun I've ever had was on the way up, working my backside off to build a real business. I might just start over and do that again. And you wouldn't know anything about that because work, to you, is nothing but political strategy to get people to admire you. That's why you'll fail one day. I don't give two beans what people think of me. All I care about is respect and hard work."

Dellwood's imposing figure was still real and powerful to Seth, and his words had hit where Seth was most vulnerable. He felt nauseated, a big knot of shame caught in his throat. Just then the phone rang. Nicolai was on the other end. "Seth, just wanted to tell you we got the goods. I have the map and the key and we start our search this afternoon."

"Well, well," Seth breathed out with a sigh. His throat was still tight but this was very, very good news. *I'll show that dreadful old man what I can do. Even if he isn't here to see it. In the end, I will win.*

Chapter 34

The meeting with the governor and representatives from several other islands had started off badly. No one knew where Kit had gone and Ian had been forced to start the meeting without her. Two hours of listening and clarifying had gone by while the four of them asked their questions, and Addie was feeling fairly confident they'd be able to work through the leadership problems the conservatory had experienced thus far. The biggest issue facing them now was the apparent lack of resources, which made the hotel company's offer tempting. After hanging up with Leigh, she knew the hotel chain might not end up with the resources, either, so she was looking for creative options that would empower and resource the local leadership. With Nate's help as a leadership consultant, the islanders would become much more organized and effective simply by learning how to collaborate. Change necessitated new sets of skills and Addie was making a list of the skills they'd need. *We're not born knowing how to manage and lead.* Because of their conviction and clarity about what they wanted, she held much hope for them. She and Ian had missed the strengths they'd hoped for from Kit, but had facilitated very well together despite her absence. Jim was extremely helpful with the communication planning and had also contributed missing pieces and ideas they'd need to spread the word.

As the meeting drew to an end at 4 p.m., the team shook hands with their new friends and agreed to meet again in three days. All had their assignments and would focus on their parts of the plan. Nate looked lighter and more hopeful as he smiled in appreciation and bid them goodbye, then walked over the ridge to his home. The other three stayed behind to share a drink and celebrate the end of a positive intake meeting.

Jim was first to mention the obvious. "Hey, where the heck is Kit, does anyone know? That gal can be so unpredictable sometimes!"

"I thought you both knew," said Addie. "I was on the phone when she left, so I thought you two had sent her on an errand or something." She looked at Ian, who now appeared worried.

"Hmmm, I really don't know. And I haven't been on land with her enough to know if she does disappearing acts as a habit."

Jean Claude heard the end of this conversation as he returned from the men's room. "Me either. She said she was going for a walk for some fresh air before the meeting."

Jim wondered if Kit had gone looking for that map and key, but didn't say anything because he wasn't ready to out her.

"Well, drink up," Ian said. "I think we'd better walk over the hill and see if anyone has seen her over in Old Wall. There's only one street and not very many places to go, so they'll know." Ian pushed back his chair. The four of them stood and found their way down the beach to the opening in the palms where the path led over the ridge to the village. It was still hot and they were dripping wet within minutes. Over the hill, they started down the road to Old Wall and stopped in the first small restaurant. The owner was bright-eyed and smiling. "How can we help you?"

Ian said, "We're looking for a woman who might have walked by here earlier today. Easy to notice because she has a head of red hair."

"Nope, no one like that came over the ridge today. Would've seen her. Quite sure of it."

"Is she the woman who was at the tavern with all of you this morning?" A small voice came from the dark shadows next to the bar. Marissa sat with her cousin at a small table, peeling shrimp.

"Why yes, her name is Kit. Have you seen her?" asked Addie.

"Not here in the village," answered Marissa. "But while I was sitting on the beach at my break, I did see her get into your dinghy and head to your boat. She seemed in a hurry, which I thought was strange."

"I think I know what she was doing." Jim glanced at Addie and decided to spill the beans, since Kit was missing. "And if she was doing what I think, she may be trying to find the key and the map."

Addie frowned. "She's probably just on the boat looking for them. Right, Jim?"

Jean Claude's face looked concerned. "Why was she after the key and map? What was she planning?"

Marissa's heart skipped a few beats as she listened. She was right. This was the man who came to search the caves four years ago. And that meant *he* was the one who'd caused her such heartache. She peered at him cautiously but didn't say a word.

Ian said, "We'd better get to the boat and see if we're right, Jean Claude." His voice was urgent. "She's been gone for hours now, and there's no telling what could have happened if she took the tender by herself."

The four of them rushed out of the restaurant, leaving Marissa's head spinning. *What should I do?*

She knew why the cave was so important and she knew why they said 'it' wasn't there. Onandi's brother had moved it to the secret cave you could only reach by going underwater through the cave on the south side. And the wheel had been moved to an even more secret place that only she and Onandi knew about. *Her precious... Onandi. Oh, how she missed him. This man's desire for the ship's treasures had caused Onandi's brother to die. And now they were both lost to her.*

Marissa ran up the ridge and down to the beach at Saltwhistle Bay. She watched as the four tourists hitched a ride from Nevil, one of the local fishermen. She decided to head straight for the old cave location from the map, to see if the woman was there. She finished up her chores for her cousin, washed her hands in the basin out back, put on a pair of pink flip-flops and hurried out the door.

Chapter 35

Jim felt uneasy. It wasn't his nature to confront conflict head-on but rather to avoid it at all costs. They'd gotten Kit in trouble and they'd be in trouble as well, because they'd been scheming together. More than anything, he didn't feel it was his place to judge others. Mainly because HE didn't like being judged himself. So he liked staying neutral in almost everything. If he put a stake in the ground on an issue, someone wouldn't like him and he couldn't tolerate that. It was a strategy that had worked all his life. He was good at reading the tea leaves and spinning the situation so everyone would like him. Lack of harmony was intolerable to him. He loved being the lighthearted guy who could brighten up even the dimmest scenario with a little laughter. It always worked. He'd always been popular with everyone and prided himself on being able to get along with everyone.

Until lately. Somehow people had started wanting more from him and he didn't know how to deliver what they expected. He hated delivering bad news and avoided it like the plague. He also avoided giving feedback and was always the one to give others the benefit of doubt. If no one else was to blame, then maybe no one would ever point the finger at him. But lately, his strategy hadn't been working. Nate's words gnawed at his very core. The skills that had served him so well were now the very things bringing him down. His playful nature was being seen as nonchalance. That was the word that made him cringe during Nate's dialogue. Who would want to follow a leader who was *nonchalant* and not convicted to a strong purpose of some kind? Jim wondered if he'd ever stood for anything. In college he started out that way, but somehow during the partying and fun, his attention had shifted to his natural ability to perform and entertain. He was the elegant and diplomatic chameleon. He naturally mirrored others and became what they needed. He knew this about himself and avoided being pinned down on any one point. Problem was, he was plagued with feelings of shame. Every time he caught himself flattering someone when he didn't really mean it. His automatic impulses were starting to embarrass him.

Nate had said, "If everyone likes you, then you'll know you don't stand for anything of your own." And, "If you know who you are, you'll know what to do." Those words had penetrated his charade and he could see how superficial he'd been, how needy for others' approval.

Addie interrupted his thoughts, "Jim, are you okay? We've got to tell them exactly what Kit was thinking, don't you see that?"

"I just don't want to betray Kit when she's not here to defend herself, you know?" Jim said this with enough hesitancy in his tone that Addie went in for more.

"No, I don't see that, Jim. We're the only ones who know the truth and we've got to tell them so we can find her. We don't know this island and, if she decided to go by herself, it could be dangerous over where the cave is. Ian said that's the windward side where the ocean is more treacherous. But we've got to be in this together, so are you in?" Addie pushed mostly due to the worrier in her.

"I dunno, Ad, I just don't know. I'm confused right now. She's probably okay and will wander back later. She's a big girl. She can take care of herself. And they'll think badly of us for scheming with her."

"Well, if you aren't with me, then I guess I'll have to tell them myself. I don't care if Kit is mad at me later. Or if they get mad at us for going along. She could be in danger!"

Jim blinked his eyes and looked over at Addie. His conscience kicked into gear. Something felt good about what she was saying. It might even be a good thing if Kit was mad at him. Somehow, it felt right, as if all of the gears in a clock clicked into unison and told him what time it was. *Moral compass.*

Pay attention to what your conscience is saying to you. Do the right thing. Even if it's going to make them mad or make them not like you. What matters is Kit's safety and right now we have to come clean about our secret meetings and the cockamamie plan Kit had underway. I have to let go of any other motives. "You're right, I should care more about her safety than whether she'll be mad at us later. Got it. Okay, who's going to tell them?" Jim liked the tone of his own voice. He liked it very much.

Chapter 36

Nicolai approached the windward side of the island in the Viking and peered through the binoculars for what might be an entrance to the bat cave indicated on the map. He knew he was close. The handwritten clues on the side of the map were taking him to this exact spot. The writing on the parchment was ancient and hard to read, but he'd purchased special archeological lenses for that purpose. This had to be it.

"Go lower the anchor and get the tender lowered, Brutus." The man cut his eyes to Nicolai, who was aware he didn't like the stupid nickname. Not saying a word, he moved to the controls that powered the electric windlass, lowering the anchor. Once set, the large boat began to sway back and forth in the strong winds. The waves bounced roughly against the sides, making the deck a precarious place to stand. The huge man held on as he walked aft to lower the smaller tender, which both men jumped into and headed for shore.

"There it is! The cave entrance." Nicolai ordered, "Slow down so we can tie up on that rock over to the side."

Brutus answered with a low "harrumph."

"Get out the fins and snorkel so we can inch through the tunnel and into the cave."

Brutus brought out the equipment and they both pulled on their gear. Within minutes they were in the water, swimming toward the entrance and into the tunnel where the surging waves pulled them back and forth until they were inside. When they surfaced, Nicolai heard a scream. Marissa, perched on the side of the cave just inside the entrance, had been surprised by the unwelcome guests. She was expecting a woman.

"Well, well. Look what we have here, Brutus. Another little extra bonus. Maybe this one can be yours if you don't screw this up!" He grabbed her by the ankles, knocking her to the ground in one swift yank and dragging her over the rocky ledge into the water. "What are you doing here young lady?" he asked with a sinister smile. Marissa clutched her blouse in her hands and said nothing, her eyes round circles of fright, but when Brutus reached to grab her, she started kicking madly. One foot smacked him in the side of the face and Brutus exploded with anger, clutching her in his huge arms and pulling her underwater until she was barely moving.

"You stupid fool, what are you doing?" screamed Nicolai. "We might need her later! We don't even know why she was here. Pull her up!"

Brutus pulled her limp body up out of the water and threw her onto the rock's ledge on the side of the cave. Marissa whimpered and cried intermittently.

Nicolai was already focused elsewhere, wildly searching this part of the cave for the chest. *The key has to be to an old chest.* The clues on the map indicated the smallest part of the cave under the tunnel and up the other side. *Where is that?* The light on his mask shone down through the dark water to an opening about forty feet away. He held his breath and dove down. He made it about halfway when he surfaced for one more breath of air and then he was gone. Ten minutes went by. Brutus was beginning to get restless.

Just then Nicolai popped up to the water's surface. He swam to the ledge and hoisted himself up.

"There's NOTHING in that cave. And it looks as though someone has been living in there so if there ever WAS anything in there, it's certainly gone now." Nicolai spit his words out in rage. *What was I thinking? How could any treasure still be around after centuries had gone by? Was I daft? DAMN. I needed that booty. If my father had only had the nerve to go after it in his lifetime, then maybe…* "Let's get the girl back to the boat and then we'll think about what's next." Looking at his large companion, he blurted out, "Don't you have a tongue? Why don't you ever speak?"

Brutus didn't utter a word, which made Nicolai fume even more. Holding Marissa to his chest, Brutus dropped his big body into the water and started swimming back to the boat. Nicolai swam after him, dejected and full of rage at his father, who was certainly to blame for his not finding what he was entitled to. His family should have been wealthy beyond imagination, but the women had kept the secret from the men for so many years. *And now it is too late.*

Nicolai and Brutus boarded the Viking and dragged their new find onto the deck, then down below into the cabin. Brutus taped her mouth shut and unlocked the door to the cabin where Kit lay quietly on the bunk. Marissa stared at the other woman as the door latched behind her, then moved over to the bunk next to Kit and turned her back so her fingers could pull the tape from Kit's eyes and mouth. Kit yelped as the tape came off but was glad to be able to see again. Marissa then carefully pulled the tape from Kit's hair and mouth. Kit rose to return the favor, and the two women spoke quietly.

"Who are you?" Kit asked. "And what just happened?"

"My name is Marissa. I live here on the island. Your friends were looking for you and I wondered if you were trying to find the cave from the map. I knew where it was, so I came to see if you were here. They said you'd been gone for hours, and I was worried you'd hurt yourself. Very powerful waves crash into the cave opening every few minutes, so it's difficult to get in. I've been going there for years, and I thought I could help. I was waiting for you when these men found me."

"Where did you see my friends and how long ago was it?" Kit was hopeful.

"Not long ago. They went to your yacht first, to get their dinghy."

"Dinghy? What's that?"

"Oh, I think you call it the tender. The small boat you use to come to shore. They took the dog back to the yacht, too."

"Were they coming to find me?" Kit asked.

"I guess so. They seemed worried, so they're probably on their way here now, if they know the way."

"Oh, no! I have the map. They'll never know where I am now!"

"I think the Frenchman knows where it is," said Marissa, her eyes sad. "He came here a long time ago."

"Really? Jean Claude? Hmmm. So he'll know the way? Good. Maybe there's hope they'll see this boat and bring help?"

"I hope so." Marissa said with very little life left in her. She was shaken to the bone.

Kit sensed that the girl might be in a bit of shock. "Well, Marissa, you need to lie down." Kit turned around and, with her tied hands, draped a boat blanket she'd found in a locker over the soaking wet girl. "Just one more question and then I'll figure out what we need to do. Marissa, what was in that cave?"

Hesitantly, Marissa gazed up at the redheaded woman. She didn't know if she could trust her. This had been their secret for so many years. She, Yinny, and Onandi. They knew all the underwater caves and had found the booty from an old pirate ship five years ago. They'd also found the ship's wheel and other treasures in the cave on Petit Byahaut. Marissa thought about the lore she'd heard for years. Miss Rose, who owned most of Mayreau, told the story of an ancestor, a woman privateer for the French Navy. When her ship had sunk here, some of the crew had loaded what they could into a small boat and made it to Mayreau. Most had been forced to swim, some battered to death on the north shore rocks, others drowned, and still others eaten by sharks as they tried to make it to shore. Those who survived told the story of the great fire-haired woman who was their captain. She had sailed the ocean and commanded the vessel called the *La Bagourt*. The brave and adventurous Jeanne de Saint Hilaire had been one of the rare women of the sea, commissioned by the King of France so she didn't have to disguise herself like the women who had turned to piracy. She had commanded with respect and had been loved by her officers and crew. *Maybe this redheaded woman has something to do with that story? Why is she here and does she know about the ship's wheel?* "There is nothing in that cave," Marissa said. She suddenly felt nauseated. The engine had started up and the windlass was pulling up the anchor chain. The big boat lurched in the bouncing surf.

180

Kit pushed. "But there *was* something in that cave, wasn't there? I can see it in your eyes."

"A long time ago…"

"And you saw it, Marissa? What was it? Where is it now?"

Years of keeping a secret from her family had taken its toll on Marissa. She wanted to unburden herself. She wanted someone to know. And for some reason, she liked this woman. "The wheel, the ship's wheel was there. And a chest."

"A treasure chest?" Kit was excited.

"Yes, it is supposed to contain jewels from Africa but we did not have the key to open it. The boys tried to get into it, but it was very heavy, rusted shut from many years of being underwater, and covered with barnacles. The boys hid it in the underwater cave. But the wheel, that's what I love. It's somewhere else."

"The wheel? Why do you love it, Marissa? What's so special about it? And where is it?"

Marissa's desire to be free of her secrets overcame her desire to keep them. "It's in a bat cave at Petit Byahaut, in St. Vincent," she confided.

The boat roared out to sea and crashed onto the waves, knocking Kit to her knees and cracking her head on a cabinet edge. Momentarily frightened, she picked herself up and crawled onto the bunk with Marissa so they could talk without being heard. Her head pounded and her forehead was already starting to swell.

"I love it because it is beautiful," Marissa said wistfully. "It has big green and red and yellow and orange jewels all around the edges. And it has lovely words carved into it. We were told it held the secret to commanding on the high seas, that Captain de Saint Hilaire carved the words into the wheel and the crew lived by the virtues in those words. They believed they were blessed with good wind, good currents and good fortune because of them." Marissa's eyes shone brightly as she spoke.

"So, that's what all of these clues were about." *I just knew it. There is a treasure after all. I can't wait to tell Jim and Addie my instinct was rock solid. I'm always right. When are people going to admit that?*

"Where is the chest, Marissa?" Kit was after the treasure, less interested in the sacred wheel.

"The only person who can show you is no longer here. My parents won't let me dive anymore, so I cannot take you there. My ears have problems if I go too deep, and the cave where the chest is located is south of Mayreau and very deep."

"Who's the person who can take me, Marissa? Tell me now. This is important," Kit insisted.

"His name is Onandi. He left the island four years ago after his brother was killed taking the Frenchman to the cave. He has disappeared and I don't know where he is." Tears formed in her eyes. "He's been gone since then."

"Is there anyone who might know where he's gone?"

"If I knew, I would have gone after him myself." Marissa was openly crying now and the words caught in her throat.

"Okay, okay, now. Calm down." Kit wasn't exactly comfortable with emotions, and turned her head away to think while she gave the girl a moment to get herself together.

Just then the boat roared to a full stop and swung around in a circle. Brutus opened the cabin door with a jerk, grabbed Marissa off the bunk, and pulled her into the parlor.

Nicolai slammed the cabin door shut and began interrogating Marissa. "Where the hell is it? What was in that cave belongs to me and you'd better tell me what you did with it. Have you moved it somewhere? You'd better tell me if you don't want to end up being shark bait by the end of the day. I'm sure they'd love a tasty evening meal, don't you think, Brutus?" He smirked.

Marissa held her chin up in defiance and sat without speaking. She would *never* tell this man where the wheel was. Maybe the chest, but only if it meant her life. She didn't care about the chest as much as the boys had. Maybe she would take them to the chest. Onandi had been gone for so long, what did it matter now?

"Spit it out, NOW!" Nicolai grabbed her long braids, yanked her head back, and screamed at the young girl, "Don't look at me with such defiance. You'll regret it, I can assure you!" Brutus pulled out a switchblade and started toward her.

"All right. I'll take you there," Marissa said, nearly choked with fear. She'd never known men with such evil in their eyes. "But you must have dive equipment."

"No problem," Nicolai said, his tone determined. "We have dive equipment and tanks on-board. Let's go! What are the headings?"

"I don't know, but I can take you there."

"Well, get up to the helm and get us there quickly. We don't have much daylight left and we don't want to wait until tomorrow."

Chapter 37

Back on the *True Tilt,* Ian and Jean Claude had gathered up their dive gear and thrown it into Nevil's boat. The map and key were indeed gone. Jim had come clean and told them Kit was expecting to find treasure and was probably off on a hunt of her own making. The four of them would go to the cave site and look for her with Nevil's help. Ian had radioed a message to Nate, who would stay on alert on shore.

The wind picked up as they rounded the top corner of the island's north shore, and they crashed into the surf. Ian pulled to a full stop as he caught sight of the large Viking tied up outside the cave.

Addie cried out, "That's the boat I saw several times following us all the way from Tortola! It gave me a creepy feeling."

"Sheesh, Addie, "said Ian. "You should have reported it to me if you were worried about it. Our safety is important."

"I felt ridiculous telling you because I didn't know if I was imagining things."

"Well, next time, tell that intuitive rascal inside you to pipe up, Ads! You've got some serious radar."

They pulled up behind a large boulder and waited. After a few minutes they saw two men swim out to the tender and motor back to the Viking, the larger of the two dragging a woman roughly up on deck.

Jean Claude whispered, "It's that girl from the tavern, who told us she'd seen Kit. What is she doing here? Those men look dangerous." The four stayed hidden and followed the boat when it rounded the point back to the leeward side of the island.

They passed Saltwhistle Bay, headed around Col Point and beyond Saline Bay on the southern half of Mayreau. Jean Claude realized where they were headed. Remembering where he'd lost Jane, he felt dizzy with an almost physical blow. He knew he'd probably come back on this trip but he hadn't expected this emotional impact. It had been four years. Steeling himself against the memories, he narrowed his eyes and looked toward the horizon. *We're going there whether I'm ready or not.*

The Viking was anchored at the exact spot Yinny had taken him and Jane. He'd recorded the latitude and longitude, but the boy had quite accurately gauged the location using visual markers. Sixty feet below the spot would be the mouth of the underwater cave.

With binoculars, they could see the large man watching guard on the deck of the Viking, the tattoos covering his arms now visible. The boat was swinging slowly back and forth with the wind. A black dock line hung from the swim platform. Ian thought it would be too dangerous to approach openly, so he rounded the island close to shore and hid their boat just out of sight. He knew the other entrance to the cave came out only thirty yards from shore.

There were no police on Mayreau, so it was up to them to neutralize the situation, whatever it was. Jean Claude sent Nevil to town on foot to notify some of the men that a woman was missing and they needed help. He was also to tell Nate about the current situation. Then Jean Claude and Ian quickly put on their dive gear and submerged just offshore. They'd catch whoever was down there by surprise from the other end of the cave. He suggested that Jim and Addie hide in the boat or in the palm trees on shore.

Jean Claude fastened the end of the safety line to a large rock at the mouth of the cave before entering. The two turned on their forehead lights and made their way down the long narrow entry tunnel to the deeper section where the man was likely to be. There were several turns in the cave, so the safety line would be critical for a safe return. Twenty minutes later, Ian's hand stopped

Jean Claude from advancing. There was commotion ahead of them, two divers dragging a chest to the far wall of rock just beneath the mouth of the cave. One of them was tying a line to one handle and then over to the other handle. It was difficult to tell exactly what they were doing, because the turbulence had stirred up silt from the bottom and substantially reduced visibility. A few minutes later, the larger diver yanked the line and the chest began to rise to the mouth on the deep end of the cave.

Ian and Jean Claude were perched on a ledge at a higher elevation, so they hadn't been noticed as they came into the cavernous "room" of the biggest and deepest part of the cave. Jean Claude's hand instinctively rested on the dagger in his ankle strap. The one his father had given him that had been passed down through many generations. Remembering the sight of Yinny in the mouth of the shark, he had to control his rising fear. *Not now, I have to stay calm.*

Visibility was declining rapidly, but they could see the two divers struggling with one another. Jean Claude caught a view of the larger diver cutting the regulator hose of the smaller diver, who appeared to be the island girl. She tried to swim up to the cave entrance but he pulled her back and pushed her down with his feet, then swam away quickly.

Jean Claude's instincts kicked into gear and he made a split-second decision, pulling his dagger from its sheath and cutting his own safety line, then plunging into the chaos to rescue the girl. He couldn't allow the death of another young person here.

Ian was right behind him. Free of the safety line, the two plunged into the depths below. Jean Claude went straight for the girl, tossing his dagger to Ian, who headed for the diver who'd left her here to die. From below, Ian could see the chest had been lifted to the aft of the Viking and was being pulled on-board. It must be almost night outside, because the water had darkened substantially even outside of the mouth of the cave. The diver had risen to the surface more quickly than was safe and Ian wasn't about to risk the bends, so he checked his gauges. He wouldn't have time or enough air to reach the surface and also lead the others back through the cave to safety. Especially without the safety line. He wasn't familiar with this dive and would need the time. He headed back to J.C. and the girl, giving the hand signal that they'd need to move quickly, especially with the girl sharing air from their tanks. He checked their air gauges. Both were below 500 psi, which was close, but might be enough to get them safely to the surface.

Swimming up to the ledge, Ian found the safety line. The three of them entered the narrower section and followed the line back to the top. Every few minutes Ian would switch the girl from one octopus to the other so the air depletion was evenly distributed. The safety line was doing its job, leading them through the caves with the speed they needed. J.C.'s gauge was reading in the red zone now, so Ian took the girl onto his octopus and signaled for J.C. to surface ahead of them. His gauge was also in the red, but he'd be right behind.

At the surface, Jean Claude saw the sun had set and very little light was left. He turned on his forehead light, shone it toward what he thought was the shoreline, and gasped. Not twenty feet ahead of him Jim was floating face up in the water. As Ian surfaced, J.C. motioned for him to hurry and they rushed over to Jim's body to check his vitals. He had a pulse and was breathing, but wasn't in good shape.

"Addie!" Ian yelled, but there was no answer. The boat was gone.

To Marissa he said, "You're the girl we saw in the restaurant in Old Wall?" asked Jean Claude. "What's your name again?"

Marissa was in extreme pain from her left ear, which had popped because of the deep dive. She weakly replied, "Marissa. I was on the big boat with your friend you were looking for. I went to find her and they'd already gotten her. We were tied up in the forward cabin together."

"So, they've got Kit on the boat." Ian's teeth clenched together and the muscles under his cheeks twitched with anger. "Is she okay or have they hurt her?" He asked with firmness.

"She's okay, she's just bruised from a fall, but she's tied up pretty tight," said Marissa.

With no boat, they'd have to walk back over the big hill to town. It was now pitch-black outside and they'd need to hurry. "Come on, let's go," said Ian.

"Addie may be in trouble, too. Let's pull Jim up under the palms and cover him with palm fronds. We'll have to come back for him. Seems these men have a penchant for taking women with them, so I am guessing Addie has been abducted."

The three of them started walking, Marissa pointing to a trail that started at the end of the beach.

"Marissa," said Ian, "how did you get tangled up in this? How did you know where to go to find her?"

Jean Claude answered before she had a chance. "I think I know. You look familiar to me... were you here before when I came?"

"Yes, I met you four years ago. My friend Yinny took you to get the chest down there. He never came back. He convinced us to trust you because you had the map and he thought maybe it belonged to you. But you killed him!" Her eyes filled with tears.

"Marissa, I'm so sorry. I didn't kill him, I tried to *save* him. We had an O-ring blow and Yinny was injured down there in the cave. It was an accident. He was bleeding and we were almost to the boat when a shark attacked us and carried him to the bottom. I dove over and over trying to find him and pull him to the surface. I dove down so many times, I lost my wife." Jean Claude was somber.

"Your wife died? But you took her to the hospital in Grenada! We never saw you again. Nor Yinny. My Onandi left looking for you and he has never come back, either." Her eyes flashed the hatred she felt for him. "He went to make you pay for his brother's death."

"Marissa, I am so sorry. It was a tragic accident and we both lost loved ones. My wife died in the hospital. I didn't realize she'd been grazed so deeply by the shark's teeth that she was bleeding into the bottom of the boat. I took so long trying to save Yinny, I allowed my wife to die. I still live with that."

Marissa softened a shred and looked at him with a side-glance. *Maybe he didn't mean to ruin our lives. I hate the tourists sometimes. They come and leave. They don't know about the trail of consequences they leave behind them. They are often careless and thoughtless.*

They walked in silence, all of them lost in their own thoughts. The sky grew darker as Marissa guided them to the lights in Old Wall.

Chapter 38

Seth couldn't believe his good fortune. He'd wisely funded the opportunistic Nicolai and his crazy scheme to charter the Viking and find the chest of jewels from Africa that had sunk somewhere in the Caribbean. Nicolai's ancestor had been a witness for the crown when the cargo was registered to *La Bagourt*, and the letter describing this had been passed down for generations, including how the beautiful ship had gone down near St. Vincent, Grenadines. In those days, they didn't have the equipment to dive deep enough to recover the valuables from a sunken ship. So it sat in the sea for centuries until Emile Gagnan and Jacques Cousteau invented the modern demand regulator and dive suit that allowed staying underwater long enough to explore sunken ships. Nicolai had a drunk for a father who could have been first to search for it once the technology was available, but was afraid to do so. Nicolai was convinced the treasure still lay beneath the sea. And he was right. This investment would change both of their lives.

The call from Nicolai came an hour ago and Seth could barely contain himself. He was on the Internet searching for black market buyers of precious jewels. The money would pay off his debts and give him the cash to settle the equity needed to close the two hotel chain deals still holding up his empire. He'd send Nicolai offshore to run the Trinidad Hotel and launder the income from the jewels and from the crops in South America. They were set for life. He would have his kingdom of hotels and his hoards of admirers.

Seth leaned back in his chair and fantasized about the speeches he'd give.

They would love him. He imagined the first conference, what he would be wearing, how he would walk up on stage so casually. His speech would be flawless, manipulating the emotions of the room with elegant ease. First they would lean forward in their seats, then he'd bring tears to their eyes, and last, they would laugh out loud. All because of his measured delivery of the right words at precisely the right moment. It was so simple to make them do what he wanted. He thought of the admiration in their eyes as they looked up at him with big smiles and loud applause. Nothing could replace this feeling. At the end of the speech, they'd all want to touch him. The high he'd feel would last for a few days. He wished it could last longer because of what came after it.

He shut down his computer and went to his huge, custom-made closet to select a suit from the long row of custom-made clothes. There was time to find the right buyer tomorrow. Tonight he had a dinner to attend.

Chapter 39

Nate had called to the mainland in Grenada for reinforcements, to help find Kit and to find out what the men on the Viking were up to. Violence was unheard of in Mayreau so the officials were surprised, but they promised to send an equivalent boat and also officials from the Royal Grenada Police Force, which regulated marine affairs in the lower Caribbean. They were waiting in the Bay when Nevil arrived with news of the happenings on the south side of the island. A description of the 60-foot Viking was recorded as the target, and knowing a local girl had been abducted gave them cause to search the boat if they found it. One of the four justices of the peace was summoned to track down the identity of the girl, who may have been reported missing. Her family would have to be notified.

The RGPF left port and sped out to sea to begin the search.

~~~

Nicolai was elated. He'd struck gold. The ancient chest was so heavy they had to use a winch to bring it up from the depths, and it was difficult to open. Brutus had chipped away at the barnacles for over an hour before uncovering the lock so he could open it with the key. Still, he had to use a crowbar to wedge open the chest. Inside were hundreds of gold and silver coins, a two-handed golden chalice, jeweled broaches and necklaces and – most important – the emeralds and diamonds from Africa, described in the family letter. He had redeemed his family and redeemed himself. Everything was coming together now. Since Seth had commissioned his search and promised him a lead role in the Caribbean Operations, he wouldn't have to worry another day in his life. All they had to do now was find buyers. He would keep the treasures under lock and key and sell a little at a time. After giving Seth his share of course.

Nicolai congratulated himself on his cleverness, having reasoned correctly that the divers in the cave would come from the other end. He'd taken the Viking over to search for their dive site and found easy prey. They had no weapons at all and hadn't been able to defend themselves. The brunette was easy to catch, though the man had given Brutus more of a fight than he expected. Brutus had followed the man ashore alone and knocked him out. They took the woman with them, in case they needed her for information.

He'd replaced the tape on the redhead's eyes and mouth. She actually scared Nicolai with her rage when he came into the cabin after bringing the treasure up. He didn't want to see their faces or for them to see his more than once and this had angered him. He could not afford to leave a trail of any kind. Now he was forced to kill them both. He'd turn the Viking north, out to sea and then race straight back to Florida. Brutus had found two extra anchors in the forward lockers and was tying the women's legs together and their arms behind their backs. Once they were immobile he'd secure the anchors to the lines on their ankles, so when dumped into the sea they'd never be heard from again.

Nicolai wished he had time to enjoy the two women for a little while before tossing them into their big blue destiny, but he was too filled with panic to think about it. Brutus was pouting that he couldn't collect this reward either, but Nicolai enticed him with riches instead, and the man agreed they must make haste. He had to get the treasure north as quickly as possible so he could rendezvous with Seth. That would mean at least six days and nights of straight travel before they'd be out of danger. He'd planned to use one of the anchors to take care of Brutus on the last night out. Now he'd have to think of some other way to get rid of him.

Chapter 40

News of Ian, Jean Claude and Marissa's arrival on the edge of Old Wall village had reached Dennis's Hideaway, where police from Grenada were waiting. One of the boys in town had seen them and run to the tavern to report. This town was not used to such excitement, so the news traveled fast across the ridge and to the others on the main dock. The townspeople gathered to watch just outside the edge of the bay. Nate had one of the two Jeeps on the island and took his companions to Saltwhistle Bay, where they could strategize.

Obediah, Chief of the RGPF, said "Nate, we just got a report of the Viking from Bequia Island. The RGPF officer up there said it was seen going north at a very fast speed. We will need to coordinate with officials from the other islands if we are to catch them."

Nate replied, "Obe, we were just told that Addie, one of the women with us, is also missing. She and Jim were with Nevil's boat on the south side. Jim was found near the shore, unconscious but breathing. They had no way to bring him here, so left him covered with palm fronds under two large palms at the southernmost tip of the island. Can you get medical help to him?"

"Sure thing," Obe replied. "We'll send the boat from St. Vincent with a medical guy on-board."

~~~

Marissa's mother had been terrified while she was missing, and wouldn't let her leave the house. Marissa pretended to go to bed after the local medicine man poured some herbal oil into her ear, then slipped out the window as soon as she heard the heavy breathing of her mother falling asleep. She couldn't miss what was happening. She was a part of it, worried about the redheaded woman, and wanted to see it to resolution. She hurried over the ridge and found a place for herself in the crowd. Watching the Frenchman from the collection of local faces, she could hide herself, yet watch what was going on. *I've given up the location of my sweetheart's treasure. I hope he will forgive me if he ever comes home.*

~~~

Jean Claude and Ian insisted on boarding the police boat and going along to search for the women. The police chief resisted, but Ian convinced him they might be needed for information. They'd pulled up anchor and were headed out of port, four armed men scurrying about the boat attending to their duties while Ian and Jean Claude sat still. They both felt responsible for these women being caught up in this adventure that had escalated out of control.

Had he known the dangers ahead of them, Ian would never have brought them here. *What is this Viking crew up to and why are they here?* In the pocket of his cargos he fingered the compass between his forefinger and thumb. Addie had confessed the "gifts" they'd each been given and had turned the compass over to him in case it would help the project. But he couldn't even think about the project now that these two women were in trouble. And maybe Jim, too. He hoped Jim was safe by now and was going to be all right. His passion for the health of the reefs and the ecosystems had gotten them all in a mess he didn't understand. Neither did Nate, for that matter. None of them knew what might be going on.

Jean Claude looked at Ian soberly. "I have something to tell you."

"Well spill it, mate."

"Remember when I came here with Jane?"

"Sure J.C., you came here before I met you, right?"

"Yes, it was before I met you. Before I went on the Tilt Leadership adventure.

I had come here because of the map, Ian. The map that Jim brought here and Kit was searching for. I'm the one who planted the clues with each of them for my quest, before they got here." Jean Claude paused a moment before he went on. "The map and the key came from my father's desk, passed down for generations along with the diary of one of my ancestors. She was a woman privateer commissioned by King Louis XIV. A rare breed of woman for that age who refused either to dress like a man or to behave like a proper woman. She was notorious for her ways and revered by many. The King admired her powerful demeanor and it's told they may have been lovers. Though the truth of this is not known, he did grant her wish to command the seas, and she captained a royal vessel called *La Bagourt*. She and her crew set sail for the Canary Islands off of Africa and, it was told, took diamonds, rubies, and emeralds on-board, then sailed for the West Indies to add cotton, sugar, salt and other spices into the hold before circling back to France. News travelled that she was shipwrecked on the reef of Tabago Cays near here, and the ship escaped the reef only to sail to the deep side of Mayreau and sink to the bottom. She and her crew spent the rest of their lives on Mayreau."

"Gadzooks, man. What a story!" Ian was intrigued.

"That's why I came here with Jane, and why I'm back again. I've been obsessed with this family story and lost Jane because of it, fool that I am. Now my inability to resist the temptation to come here again is causing more trouble. I have to know if the ship's wheel is here. It holds the secret to my ancestor's great ability to lead. My family has old manuscripts describing how she carved her secrets into the helm of the vessel and swore to lead France to a new age of creativity and greatness. But now I again doubt my motives. Is all of this worth it? Kit, Addie, that boy Yinny who died, and especially Jane. Losing Jane made me see my insane obsession for what it was." Jean Claude hung his head as he finished his confession.

"Well, I for one am glad you're here, mate. We need your expertise on the matter of the conservancy. Your personal motives don't matter to me. Life doesn't always work out as neatly as we think and you couldn't have predicted that some bad guys would arrive just when we did. Keep your head about you. We need you to be at your best, and guilt is not useful. We must help get these people back safely. Remember the first principle of leadership? Stability comes from the leader having command of his emotions. Temperance. Composure.

If you stay calm, so will everyone else. That's the key we must remember right now mate."

"You're right, Ian. Thank you for the reminder. My father used to say that all the time." Jean Claude paused for a moment and added, "I just wanted you to know."

Ian nodded his head with approval.

The boat raced through the night air, cutting into the waves with ease. The two were starting to nod off when excited voices awakened them.

Chapter 41

The Viking had made a stop to fuel up in Kingstown on St. Vincent, the northernmost island of the lower Caribbean, and was making its way up the windward side of the island past Fort Charlotte.

Nicolai said, "Brutus, in a few minutes we should round Petit Byahaut Point, which the chart indicates is a peninsula that juts out into the ocean right where we need to head out. When we arrive at the waypoint I've set near there, we need to set a new heading which will take us out to sea. Then we can dump our unnecessary 'cargo'." He nodded his head in the direction of the women. "Do you have them ready?"

Kit's ears perked up when she heard him say "Petit Byahaut." *What meaning does that have...?* She was doing everything in her power to think her way out of this mess.

Brutus sauntered over to the cockpit where Addie and Kit were bound and tied with anchors tethered to their ankles. He checked them over one more time. He noticed a loose loop in one of the lines in Addie's binding, stuck the small switchblade into the knot to loosen it, and used both hands to grasp the small lines with his rather large fingers. Standing up, he nodded an affirmation in Nicolai's direction and went below for one last trip to the head before going out to sea. *I get nauseated being out at sea, and going below makes it worse.*

When Addie moved slightly to adjust her aching legs, the switchblade clattered loudly as it dropped to the deck under the table. He had left the knife in the knot! She felt an adrenaline rush as she prayed neither of the men heard it. She couldn't see because of the tape over her eyes, but she'd heard the steps of the man called Brutus going below deck, and she was pretty sure the other one was at the nav station plotting waypoints because she'd heard him turning charts. *Probably working on the chartplotter.* She'd have to judge whether the other man was looking her way and make her move now. She tried to remember which direction the nav station faced. *I'm fairly certain it was facing forward, which means he has his back to the rear cockpit. I have to be quiet and not call attention to myself, or we'll be dead.* Addie steeled herself and slid her bound body down onto the floor under the cockpit table. Her legs were weak from the tight lines around them, so she slipped a little while searching the floor with her hands, still tied behind her back. Moving around slowly and cautiously so as to make as little noise as possible, she leaned on her side and searched for the knife.

Kit, realizing what Addie was doing, started feeling around the floor with her feet. With the anchor tied to her ankles she didn't have much leeway, but she could feel around with her toes over a small range. Bingo! The edge of her small toe made contact with the knife and moved it ever so slightly so Addie could hear it.

Addie maneuvered herself over near Kit and picked up the knife.

Just then, she heard Nicolai get up from the nav and walk over to the galley, then the sound of the fridge door opening and shutting, crinkling paper, and the microwave door opening. Just enough noise for Addie to get her legs beneath her body and push herself back up toward the seats. Brutus returned to the cockpit and jerked her back on the seat, saying, "Don't move or you'll fall again. Not too smart! And don't think you're going to escape because there's nowhere to go but off the boat and you have anchors tied to you."

This is the most he's said in days, thought Nicolai. *Maybe the brute does have a brain.*

"We're there," Nicolai announced. "Right off the tip of this peninsula we'll head out to sea. Have you secured everything below deck, Brutus? I don't want to hear a bunch of crap slamming all over the place down there this time and making a mess. Did you tie up the coffeemaker? I'm still sliding all over the place down there from coffee grinds all over the floor."

"Yeah, everything's secure. I just looked around."

"Okay, then, here we go." Nicolai turned the wheel west and hit the gas. The engine revved, and then one moment later, coughed out a big noise and stopped. The nose of the large vessel dropped dramatically back down. Then silence.

"What happened?" Nicolai yelled, blaming Brutus who shrugged his shoulders and lifted his arms as if to say *I have no clue.* "Well, something must have happened? What did you do when you filled up the gas tanks in Kingstown, dimwit? Did you change the fuel filter too?"

"No, I didn't know I was supposed to."

"The gas down here is crap sometimes, so you have to check the fuel filter, you idiot. If our engine has stopped working, I'm going to kill you! Get down there and check it."

"I don't know where it is. You're the one with some boat experience."

"I'll show you where it is, but you'd better fix it." Nicolai rummaged through the nav station bookshelf to find the engine operations manual. An hour later, the two of them were still in the engine room up to their elbows in black grease. Between the two of them, they had not been able to figure out the problem.

Chapter 42

They'd just received a report from Kingstown, where the Viking had refueled and stocked with water. Ian could now see the large white boat through binoculars he'd found at the nav station. He lost sight of it for a moment, and then steadied his arm to find it again. Lights were shining in the cockpit at the stern, making it visible in the dark. The full moon shone brightly as well.

"I see them!" Ian could also see that the two women were tied up and a large man was moving about the stern near them.

He passed the binocs to Jean Claude, who took over while Ian conversed with one of the police officials. "We've got to get over there quickly! Are you equipped to board that boat and take possession? It seems to be stopped for some reason."

"We know," said the officer. "The dockmaster in Kingstown heard our broadcast and added water to their fuel. That boat is not going anywhere."

Just then Jean Claude jumped up and yelled, "They've dropped one of the women off the stern of the boat with an anchor tied to her!! Oh my God. Get over there. Now!" J.C. was clearly panicked. Closing the few hundred yards between them, they arrived just as Brutus dumped the second woman over the stern.

While the armed officers boarded the Viking and captured the two men on-board. Jean Claude and Ian dove off their boat, down where the women had entered the water. It was pitch black.

Beneath the surface, Addie held her breath and steadied herself against the panic threatening to engulf her. The switchblade was tucked in the back of her shorts and she prayed she and Kit wouldn't drop so far they'd drown anyway. Falling, falling, she tried to stay upright so that the knife wouldn't fall out of its secure location. Then she hit bottom. From what she could tell, they had not dropped too deep. Quickly she located the knife, clicked on the switchblade release and cut through the line holding her hands. It was freed easily and she ripped the tape from her eyes. She sawed away at the line holding the anchor to her ankles. *Thank the good lord the knife is extremely sharp.*

Frantically looking around for Kit, Addie suddenly saw Ian swimming toward her with a flashlight! She handed him the knife and motioned in the direction where Kit must have landed. Ian motioned that she should surface, and headed toward Kit. Addie gulped in air when she reached the top. *I made it to the surface!*

Just then she saw Jean Claude come to the surface for air. He quickly blurted out orders, "We've got her, Addie, get to the boat quick!" He motioned toward the police boat now rafted up to the Viking. He dove again and within minutes, Kit, Ian and Jean Claude all came to the surface in one huge gasping trio. Addie breathed a huge sigh of relief. *They got her free in time.*

The crew of the Viking was in custody and being held in handcuffs. The police searched the boat and confiscated the chest full of ancient treasure. The four men hooted with glee to see such an amazing booty drug up from the bottom of the sea. "Wait until the governor sees this!" one of them said. Another asked, "Does anyone know where they found this?"

"In a cave on Mayreau," said Jean Claude. "It's been there in the possession of some local youths for a few years now, so we'll need to bring it back there."

Kit said, "There's more than just that chest, Jean Claude. Marissa told me of a ship's wheel covered in jewels, too. I'm trying to remember where she told me it is. The kids found it a few years ago in some other cave. I'm racking my brain but I can't remember."

"The *wheel*? Are you *sure* Kit? Mon Dieu, if you are right, I have finally found what I have spent my life searching for. Kit, you've got to try to remember!" Jean Claude was pacing in excitement.

"Well, when we get back to Mayreau, we can ask Marissa herself," Kit answered. She knows where it is and loves it. I'm quite sure she can take us to it."

Ian and Jean Claude turned to look at one another and smiled. *Could it be?*

The engine started up and they headed back to Kingstown, the captain radioing ahead, "After we pass around Petit Byahaut, we'll be on our way. Over and out."

Petit Byahaut, Petit Byahaut. Finally, the insight hit Kit. "Petit Byahaut... that's IT. That's where the wheel is." She jumped up to ask the captain, "Where did you say Petit Byahaut is?"

"It's right ahead," the captain said. "A small island peninsula where there's an eco-travel resort."

"Does it have a cave on it?" A smile was growing on Kit's face.

"Well, as a matter of fact, there's a bat cave located there."

"Can we go there tonight?" She was even more excited now.

"No, no, that would be impossible at night. Too dangerous. Too many rocks. We have to head back now." The engine roared as the boat pulled away from the Viking.

Kit pulled the small group of her colleagues together at the stern of the boat, so no one could hear. She told them the details of her conversations with Marissa. Jean Claude was beside himself. They decided to stay the night in Kingstown and charter a local boatboy to take them to the cave in the morning. They'd call Nate and get the exact location of the wheel from Marissa.

The four of them were filled with anticipation of what the next day would bring. Yet Addie was also quiet, thinking about how close they'd come to death. *Life can be cut short at any time... and the only emotion I have room for at the moment is gratitude.*

PART THREE

THE HEALERS

Humanity ~ The open heart compels us to
love, and the Helper becomes the Healer.

"Healing happens when we are able to transcend the limits of
our humanity for some greater purpose, while simultaneously
accepting ourselves as imperfect human beings doing the work."

-Pam Boney

Chapter 43

In exhaustion, the four of them had piled into one room to save money because Ian was the only one with cash on him, and they'd need money the next day to secure a boat and dive gear. Ian awoke at the first crack of dawn, well before the others, and walked to Greaves, the local market and office, for charter boat service. He'd secured a small boat, reserved dive gear in the dive shop at Petit Byahaut and collected information about the bat caves. To make swift time of their departure on this excursion, he'd bought baguettes and cheese for breakfast. Ian's demeanor was usually a happy one, but the bounce in his step today was particularly lighthearted. If what he'd learned was true, this cave was home to fruit-eating bats, believed to be the only ones of this species in the world, possibly less than 5000 of them left and all located here. Ian had been a naturalist all his life and he was elated with this surprise bonus – the opportunity to see these unusual bats! When he returned to the room they'd rented at the Heron Hotel on Bay Street, he called out "Up and at 'em, everyone!"

Jean Claude was first to jump up. His face looked like it was Christmas morning and he was eight years old. "Let's get up and go!" He was anxious to see the ship's wheel.

Kit stretched her arms out and yawned widely. Next to her and smashed beneath one of Kit's outstretched arms, Addie opened one eye and said lazily, "I think I want to sleep late..." She grinned and winked at Kit.

"Yeah, I'm tired too," Kit played along. " I think I want to sleep a little longer." She winked back at Addie.

"No way!" chided Ian playfully. "You gals get up off your anchor-laden butts and out of that bed!"

"Okay, okay…" Kit acted like a reluctant teenager. She jumped up and headed into the bathroom, Addie right behind her, and peered into the mirror to check the damage from sleeping on wet hair all night. Her wild tresses of chestnut brown hair were completely out of control. But, strangely enough, she didn't have a single moment's care over it. *I sure have changed in the last few weeks. All I want is a toothbrush.* Instead, she joined the others in tearing off some bread and cheese. *This will do as a substitute. And coffee… I want coffee!*

"I have a boat and dive gear reserved for all of us," said Ian. "Yellowmon, the boat boy who will take us, knows the caves and dive sites where most people go. It's an advanced dive plan, so I hope you guys are all up to it. I know you're all certified, from your paperwork coming aboard *True Tilt*. Addie, you've only done a couple of dives at resorts, so you'll need to stick pretty close to me and the dive master. Kit and Jean Claude, you have a lot of dive experience, so you'll be fine."

Addie started feeling a little nervous. She'd been on half a dozen dives, but so much time had passed she didn't remember all the rules. She tried to reassure herself that she was with experienced divers. The last time she'd gone, it was getting ready and waiting in the water, suited up in all of the gear, which made her nervous. Once she started the dive, her mind would become preoccupied with the beautiful marine life, and she'd forget her nerves.

Within ten minutes the four had finished their breakfast, checked out of the hotel and were boarding the small boat with Yellowmon, the boat "boy" with yellow hair who looked more like a man than a boy to Addie. She'd convinced them to stop for a quick coffee in Greaves. Then they'd headed straight to the ferry dock where the boat waited for them.

Ian had just received a return message from Nate with the location of the wheel. Marissa had gladly given him the information. She'd said she wanted the wheel back in Mayreau anyway, to see it again and have them place it in the little church on the top of the hill. Nate had promised he'd do his best, but it would be in the custody of the Grenadines Police, along with the chest they'd bring back that day.

Yellowmon cranked up the engine and the boat roared out of the bay and north to Petit Byahaut. He explained that the peninsula was considered an island because it was only approachable by sea. They'd have to pull into the small Buccament Bay and pick up their dive gear there at the dive shop.

Once geared up, the five of them watched as Yellowmon rounded the corner to the next headland to the west, wound along the shore, then looked as though he were going to crash the boat right into the foliage. But beneath the overhanging palms and brush was a shallow tunnel that led into the island. Yellowmon proceeded slowly through the overhanging limbs, telling everyone to lean down into the boat to avoid getting their heads knocked off. After a while he stopped the boat and said, "Here's where we get off and start the dive. Is everyone geared up? You're going to need to drop off the boat back-first. It's about 30 feet deep here, so don't worry. The plan is to move along the tunnel a little farther through very shallow water so this is as far as the boat goes. You'll need to manage your buoyancy carefully. You'll weave your way through the rocks, letting the surge float you over and around the rock formation. Ian, you'll be fascinated that the ceiling is fractured in triangles as if planned. Once through that section you're into the big fissure. There the water drops to 40 feet and the fissure rises up to 30 feet where the bats live. Ian, if you want to see the bats again, we can go back after the dive is over. Everyone ready?"

Addie's stomach was flipping over on itself. *Drop over the side on your back?* She hadn't done that before. Struggling to pull their fins over their feet, they all looked so silly and awkward she'd been able to laugh a little. She watched as Ian, Yellowmon and Kit dropped off the sides of the boat like experts anxious to see something exiting. Jean Claude was waiting and watching after her, which she appreciated immensely. She didn't want to be last.

Jean Claude gently helped her ease back until she dropped off the side of the boat and steadied herself in the water. It was surprisingly easy. He dropped in the water then, staying right behind so he could keep an eye on her. He'd started having protective feelings for Addie a while back, so this felt natural to him and welcome to her.

The beauty of the underwater world took Addie's breath away. Quite literally. She almost forgot to breathe in from her regulator as she peered at the huge school of Blue Tangs momentarily disrupted by a couple of Yellowtail Snappers chasing them. A scorpion fish floated in front of her, while an army of squid moved in precise unison as if one body moved them. The sun sparkled off the fish and radiated through the water like an underwater rainbow. She'd never seen anything more beautiful.

The others had moved ahead and entered the fissure. Coral, sponges and fans sprouted from the bottom and walls of the tunnel in brilliant colors. Jean Claude pointed to a lobster poking his head out of a hole in the coral wall. Ian was lingering to gaze up through the large triangle of rock where thousands of St. Vincent bats and hundreds of Fisher Bats lay contrasted against the blue fissure and black rock. Addie and J.C. gently kicked their fins harder to catch up with the others who had moved into the next room of the cave. Addie watched J.C. wait for a surge of rushing water from the Oceanside opening to fill the narrow passage allowing it to fill in order to make the passage over the spot. She held her breath and waited for the next surge to take her over too.

On the other side of the fissure there was a sudden drop down into a small canyon with two very large boulders at the bottom. A multitude of fish varieties darted around the protected area and created the picture of a thriving system of life that seemed surreal. Yellowmon led them forward to the place Ian had told him about. Down through the space between the two boulders was another, narrow tunnel entrance hidden by the largest of the two boulders. It didn't look big enough for a human body, but they'd learned it was indeed possible to enter, though a very tight fit to squeeze their bodies through. Addie was a little concerned one of them would get cut by the coral on the sides of the tunnel and hesitated until J.C. motioned her forward. With a bravery she didn't know she had in her, she went forward confidently. Everyone had made it through to the other side, so she carefully inched her way along the tunnel, using her gloved hands to keep from bumping into the sharp edges of rock. She emerged into a small room of rock, Jean Claude the last to enter behind her. They were still underwater, beckoned by daylight from above. Yellowmon led them to the surface slowly, taking a five-minute stop. As Addie surfaced and peeled off her mask, she exhaled and looked to the west to see what everyone was staring at. There it was. Upon a ledge on one side of the room, the ship's wheel leaned against the rock wall. The jewels around the spokes of the wheel reflected the sunlight in reds, greens and yellows, their reflections from the shimmering water bouncing around the room.

The five of them grew silent, in awe of the wheel's grandeur. Especially Jean Claude.

Chapter 44

They were headed back to Mayreau in the police boat, to turn the treasures over to the Grenadines Government. News of the recovery of the ancient Mayreau treasures, especially the ship's wheel, had spread quickly throughout the lower islands of the Grenadines.

Brother King had called Ian from Old Hegg Turtle Sanctuary and asked him to request a stop on their way back to Mayreau. He had an apprentice from Mayreau who wanted to go home with them. Brother said the youth was one of the boys who'd originally found the wheel in Petit Byahaut four years earlier, and had information about it to report to the local authorities. The officials stopped the boat to pick the young man up in Admiralty Bay and were delighted to hear the story of his finding the wheel. Jean Claude recognized him as one of the boys who'd been in the tavern when he hired Yinny four years earlier. He'd introduced himself as Onandi.

"Onandi, how long have you been living in Bequia?" Jean Claude asked carefully.

"Four years, almost." He answered with very little emotion in his voice. He wouldn't look at Jean Claude.

"I think I knew your brother, Onandi."

"Yes, you are right. I know who you are. I went looking for you," replied Onandi, his eyes cold.

"I can imagine that you did." Jean Claude sat quietly and let a few moments pass to honor what had just been said.

Onandi looked at him, surprised that the Frenchman wasn't trying to defend himself.

"My wife died two days later. It was the worst time of my life and I have regretted making the decision to go that day… almost every moment I have lived since then." He sat in silence again.

"Why did your wife die?"

"Same reason your brother did. An O-ring blew while we were down there. Yinny got scratched on the coral reef and was bleeding. My wife was sharing her air with him as we tried to reach the surface."

"Sharks can smell a drop of blood for miles," Onandi reasoned out loud. "Then what happened?"

"I hadn't even thought about sharks at that time. I was just trying to get them to the surface so we could get help for Yinny. He was bleeding and barely conscious, so he wasn't able to swim using his fins."

"What happened then?" Onandi's eyes softened ever so slightly.

"I thought we were going to run out of air, but we made it to the surface. That's when the bull shark hit. He dragged Yinny to the bottom. I got my wife onto the dive boat and then dove down to help Yinny. I must have gone back down after him twenty times, not wanting to give up. I didn't realize it until later, but the sharp teeth of the shark had also injured my wife. The back of her leg was sliced open and she bled in the boat for too long before I could have her flown to the hospital in Grenada." Jean Claude's throat tightened as he said this and he had to stop talking. Onandi noticed the emotion.

"So, your wife died, because you were trying to save my brother?"

"Yes, I'm afraid so. I'm not certain she would have lived anyway, but yes, I have questioned my actions over and over. A thousand times."

"Then you know how I feel," Onandi acknowledged, with some satisfaction in his voice.

Jean Claude couldn't continue speaking.

Ian had been listening nearby and laid a hand on his shoulder. "I think what Jean Claude is trying to say is…. we are sorry for the loss of your…"

"Wait, Ian! I need to be the one to say it." Jean Claude looked Onandi in the eye and said he was so sorry for what happened to his brother. He wished he had never made the trip at all. But he accepted it now. "Life is change."

Onandi said "I forgive you. Yinny died doing what he loved and I miss him. But I have healed from taking care of the turtles. They die too. Even after I have tried to save them sometimes. It is part of life…"

The sun shone brightly in the Caribbean sky, its warmth penetrating Jean Claude's skin. He gazed at the horizon and saw the profile of Mayreau ahead, feeling at peace for the first time in four years.

Chapter 45

"Look at the carvings on the ship's wheel," Nate observed. "There are four words carved into the front, and twelve carved at the top of each spoke between the handles."

Jean Claude read the four French words on the front out loud: "*Sagesse, Humanité, Courage, Resilience*. In English, they mean Wisdom, Humanity, Courage and Resilience. These match the words in her diary and now that we have the wheel, it gives us all of the twelve she referenced but never wrote down." He'd been studying the wheel for the past four days, since their return to Mayreau, and had brought it into the meeting room at the Saltwhistle Bay Resort for reference. The *True Tilt* team would be making their recommendations tomorrow to the Mayreau Environmental Development Organization, the Tabago Cays Marine Park and the other government officials of the Grenadines. He had been using the twelve virtues on the wheel as a guidepost for the work they were doing together to make sure their solution was balanced.

"The remaining words are equally interesting and also seem to be human virtues," Jean Claude continued. "There are forty-eight of them in total carved into the spokes. I have translated them into English for our meeting so we can refer to them in our strategic planning with the conservancy. They seem to have been carved into the wheel with three underlying each of the main four and then four supporting the twelve. It is quite intricate, but perfectly balanced and is beautifully simple on the surface. From what I can tell after studying them, together with documents in my family's history, the twelve virtues are those that create balance for citizenry within the human system. A reference to Aristotle's Golden Mean was found in her diary and implies that if all are kept in balance, they will provide the culture for artistry, creativity and transcendence of society to a higher order of accomplishment and contribution to history. It is fascinating." He was quite taken with his great ancestor's wisdom. *She was way ahead of her time.*

Nate said, "Thank you, Jean Claude, for studying up on this historical example of great leadership. The conservancy is going to need good leadership and we can certainly use these principles to help them learn how to keep the environment in balance. I'm grateful for this new, but old way of thinking!"

"Agreed!" chimed in Addie. "It's so beautifully illustrated in a circle. When I match this against everything I know that works in leadership in my world, it makes so much sense to me. I wish I'd thought of it. Looks so simple on the surface. Virtues in balance with each other! Jean Claude and I figured out that they go together *across* from each other too! Like Confidence and Trust or Integrity and Diplomacy. They're essentially dualities or polarities that must be balanced. The possibilities for application of this are endless. I will use this in every decision I make from now on." Jean Claude turned his eyes to her with what seemed to be a private challenge between the two of them. "Well, maybe not *every* decision," Addie qualified with a small smile at the corner of her lips. The two of them had gotten close working together on the wheel's implications. They'd both been fascinated. No one would ever guess the pair of them were both introverts. They hadn't stopped talking and problem-solving for days.

Jim came back to life in a huge way when he joined the other two in conversations about the virtues. "I see how we can use this model to present the public relations plan so we get the message across to the various stakeholders affected by the changes in the ecosystem here. I've been working on a very cool idea about how we can brand the message in a surprising way." Something had resonated with the youthful idealism he remembered in himself. As he thought about living with stronger virtues and integrity he felt he could rebuild his life. Just hearing the words as Addie and J.C. spoke about the virtues had ignited his creativity. Ideas for the campaign were spilling out of him, just as they did in the old days. He'd called home yesterday and his wife had been willing to talk. Hope filled him with the promise of a better future. He could feel a swell of good feelings growing within him.

Kit was her usual self. Poking fun at Addie, she said "Woman, I didn't know you had so much spunk in you! Calling the CEO of your company with such a creative plan. Leigh Merriweather must be singing in the shower today!" She laughed. Addie had been hard at work for days. She'd first surfaced problems with the financials of the Caribbean Hotel chain and notified Leigh of her suspicions. Leigh had also received an email from a company whistleblower who'd partnered with a hacker in the Miami Hotel to surface the scheme and expose Nicolai and Seth. The email from the Asian woman hadn't been considered seriously until Addie shared similar suspicions and they started putting the pieces together. Both Seth and Nicolai would be indicted for fraud, attempted murder and tax evasion, among other things. Addie had conferred with Jean Claude on the legal matters and connected him with Leigh, who'd hired him to consult on the acquisition lawsuit. Jean Claude found a loophole in the transaction and the whole thing had been stopped. Leigh and the other hotel CEOs had all escaped the sale to the private equity firm and were all back in control of their companies.

Kit volunteered her services to consult on the culture challenges that would inevitably ensue with the shift in plans. Sebastian had agreed wholeheartedly, especially to her involvement with the eco-travel chain. There were always problems to solve when change was afoot. She was very good at stabilizing actions and felt confident she could help in numerous ways. She felt a strange rush of warmth run through her as she volunteered herself for work that would not be as lucrative as she was accustomed to. The near-death experience of drowning had shifted her perspective in the past few days. What mattered to her had changed, and it felt good.

Chapter 46

It was determined that the Mayreau treasures from the chest would be kept by the governing body of the Grenadines. Local descendents of the family could keep the ship's wheel because it had belonged to the Privateer of *La Bagourt* who shipwrecked there. The family decided to keep it in the church on the hill. They would be given a way to secure and display it for all to see and enjoy. After all, it was a message intended to be shared. The treasures had solved the conservancy's biggest problems. Addie's creative plan included a way to resource the support through leveraging the treasure's value. She also proposed a plan to build a chain of eco-travel resorts and sold the idea to Leigh Merriweather. Her hotel company would sponsor an entire chain of resorts targeted at adventure eco-tourism, to attract travelers interested in learning about renewable energy sources and nature conservancy. It had been successful in the Galapagos, so why couldn't they do the same thing throughout the Caribbean? Today's educated traveler wanted to learn and eco-travel appealed strongly to the generations who would inherit the world. Leigh loved the plan and put Addie in charge of the entire project. She'd be working in the islands for many years to come and was excited about how much she'd have to learn.

Ian's eyes shone brightly as he regarded the team members who'd come so far together. Nate's appeal to him for help had seemed a daunting task with no easy solution. But now, with all of their bright minds together, look what they'd created. His heart filled with gratitude for the good people of the world who'd be able to visit and see so many species of animals that would otherwise be gone.

He was filled with the warmth of hope, healing years of worry that had caused him to pursue the science of life with such a passion. Hope. What he'd longed for, and now could start to see as a reality.

Chapter 47

Leigh Merriweather sat at her desk in the corner office of her executive suite. She held the letter in her hands and marveled at what had unfolded as a result. Dellwood, the good southern boy, had been a friend for almost twenty years. On his deathbed, he'd written her a letter that no one else knew about, describing how he regretted trusting Seth and needed her help. He told her why he'd hired Seth and, at one time, had loved him like a son. But, near the end, he'd seen the depth of the vices that had grown in his young protégé. While he lay in the hospital, Seth had not even come to see him except to try to convince him to change his will. The truth had struck him deeply and painfully. Seth was out for no one but himself. Dellwood could see that now.

He'd asked Leigh to find someone she could trust and to make sure that person was given the compass that meant so much to him. His father had given it to him and told him a soul with no moral compass is a soul with no direction. Having seen the empty soul of his protégé, he wanted someone else to carry on his father's legacy. A leader he could trust. He knew Leigh would know who to give it to.

Leigh had selected Addie after she talked with her at the awards ceremony. The top five leaders in the company had been placed at the table with the senior executives. She'd answered Leigh's questions in a way that told Leigh the compass was meant for Addie. Later, Leigh had arranged to send Addie on the leadership adventure to see what she was made of and to hopefully shape who she could become. She and Reece, Dellwood's sister, had made sure Addie got the compass. Now she smiled with anticipation, thinking about the young woman's future. She had been a good choice.

Chapter 48

Marissa had been on the town dock when the police boat arrived. When Onandi leaped off the boat, her heart raced with joy. She'd waited four years, had never given up believing he was still alive and would come home to her. The boy who'd left had returned as a man. He had run the short distance of the dock to embrace her, pausing only for a moment, to take in the beauty of the young woman before him. Then he had pulled her into his arms and wept.

~ ~ ~

Steel drums merged with the sound of laughter as the sun dropped behind the horizon on the beach at Saltwhistle Bay. Less than a week after their reunion, Marissa and Onandi had spoken their vows in the tiny church on the hill where the wheel now resided. The people of Mayreau had gathered on the beach to join in the celebration of two of their own.

Walking down the beach toward the celebration, Addie and Jean Claude joined hands. Just ahead of them, Ian tossed a ball for Barnacle who bounded joyfully back to his master for another catch. Addie smiled as Jean Claude called her attention to the gentle colors of the Caribbean sunset.

For the first time in years, Addie felt full and joyous. She'd found her place in the world. She reached into the side pocket of her long skirt and felt the warmth of the compass in her hand. In that moment she knew she would never lose her way again.

BOOK TWO coming...

The Seeker becomes the Creator.

Due out in 2011.

Manufactured By: RR Donnelley
                     Breinigsville, PA USA
                     January, 2011